I

JOHN WYCLIFFE

Dates : B., About 1325 *: D.,* 1384.

"The Gospel to the Poor"

In the Lady Chapel of Old St. Paul's, the Bishop of London, supported by other bishops and not a few barons, sat in state. The occasion was an important one, for the King's chaplain was to be tried for heresy. Suddenly there was a great commotion as into the old Chapel burst a posse of armed men, led by Lord Percy, the Marshal of England. The Bishop frowned disapproval of this invasion, but before he could speak John of Gaunt, Duke of Lancaster, entered with the King's chaplain himself. As he faced the Bishop there was no sign of fear nor shame on his face, but he stood forth, ready to defend himself.

Earl Percy was the first to speak. Turning to the venerable chaplain, standing out of respect for the bishops on the bench, the Marshal bade him be seated, saying boldly to Bishop Courtenay :

" As he will have many things to answer, he should have a seat."

There was a murmur of applause from the soldiers, in which some of the barons joined, for John Wycliffe was popular with all classes of the people. The bishop's face was black with anger as he noted the sympathy in high quarters with the heretic.

" It is against reason and the practice of courts," he snapped, " that he should sit, for he has come here to answer charges brought against him. For the time of his answer, and so long as his case is being tried, it is right that he should stand where he is."

A wordy warfare began between the bishop and the marshal in which John of Gaunt joined, and before long the wrangle became so fierce that the bishop dismissed the assembly. Probably he was glad to drop the case against Wycliffe when he found how strong were the forces on the heretic's side. For the time he dare not pit his strength against the popular champion of pure religion and freedom of conscience.

During the troublous years that followed Wycliffe became the great leader in the battle for English liberty, against Pope abroad and priest at home. He began to write tracts in the common tongue, exposing the false claims of the Pope, and contrasting the evil lives of many of the priests, monks, and friars with the teaching of the Bible. The hearts of the people of England were fired with new hope as these tracts were read secretly to them.

The Bible for the People.

By slow but sure steps Wycliffe was being led to the great work of his life. Early in his conflict with the Pope, he saw that he must do more than open the eyes of the people of England to the false teaching of the Church—he must give them the Bible itself, in their own tongue. To us there is nothing novel nor startling in this plan, but in those dark ages such a scheme was revolutionary to the last degree. Furthermore, it was monstrously wicked in the eyes of the Pope, the bishops, and the clergy. In spite of all this, Wycliffe gathered a few friends around him and set to work to translate the Latin Bible into English.

YARNS ON SOCIAL PIONEERS

BY

ERNEST H. HAYES

Author of

THE "PIONEER SERIES" OF MISSIONARY BIOGRAPHIES,
"THE CHILD IN THE MIDST," "THE CONCISE GUIDES,"
ETC., ETC.

THE RELIGIOUS EDUCATION PRESS, LTD.
WALLINGTON   SURREY

CONTENTS

First Edition	.	December,	1924
Second Edition	.	September,	1925
Third Edition	.	June,	1928
Fourth Edition	.	December,	1928
Fifth Edition	.	July,	1932
Sixth Edition	.	June,	1936
Seventh Edition	.	April,	1940
Eighth Edition	.	January,	1943
Ninth Edition	.	November,	1944
Tenth Edition	.	October,	1945
Eleventh Edition	.	November,	1948
Twelfth Edition	.	December,	1952
Thirteenth Edition	.	October,	1956
Fourteenth Edition	.	January,	1960

INTRODUCTION

"And he came to Nazareth, where he had been brought up; and, as his custom was, he went into the synagogue on the Sabbath day, and stood up for to read. . . . And when he had opened the book, he found the place where it was written:

"'The Spirit of the Lord is upon me, because he hath anointed me to preach the gospel to the poor; he hath sent me to heal the brokenhearted, to preach deliverance to the captives, and recovering of sight to the blind, to set at liberty them that are bruised, to preach the acceptable year of the Lord.'"

*   *   *   *

THE yarns in this book are based on " The Nazareth Programme " and the teaching of Jesus in its social implications. In his fourth chapter, St. Luke pictures Jesus going down to His own city, Nazareth, at an early period in His public ministry, and making what Herbert Stead has called " His programme-speech." Placing Himself in the line of prophets and social pioneers of an earlier time, Jesus used a classic Old Testament passage for the purpose of His own propaganda. " He declared Himself in favour of the under-dog every time. He said it was His special job to bring good news to the poor, to proclaim release to the prisoners, and comfort for the blind and bruised."*

The aim of the writer has been to show how, under the urge of the Spirit of the Living Christ, men have followed Him in social service. The subjects of these yarns are men and women who proved to be pioneers in applying

* " A Proletarian Life of Jesus," by F. Herbert Stead.

the teaching of Jesus as a solvent to the crying social needs of the time in which they lived. The path they blazed out in the Name of Christ has now become a broad highway, trodden by the feet of many followers of the King, but it behoves us to remember that at one time pioneers bore suffering, faced hardship, endured persecution, and in some cases lay down their lives, in social work that is now open to all.

These yarns are intended for the use of workers amongst older boys and girls, who desire to interest the young adolescents of to-day in social service, and to bring home to them in a form best suited to this period, the glorious fact that Jesus Christ calls us to adventurous service for Him among our fellows at home as well as abroad. Amid the wealth of first-class missionary material, that is deservedly having wide use among workers with young adolescents, there is a place for a book of yarns that shows Christian service at home in an equally attractive light. The yarns are not fiction, but are based on standard biographies, in accordance with the ordinary yarn method, the adventurous elements being chiefly stressed. The book is not intended for the boys and girls to read themselves. Suggestions for discussion after the yarn has been told have been included, to indicate a method rather than cover all the ground. Young adolescents love to review such yarns, to seek further information upon the subject, and to discuss motive and weigh achievement. To help leaders to answer questions and guide such discussion, biographical and other notes have been added, the aim clearly stated, and reference books given wherever possible. The yarns should never be told without an opportunity for question and discussion being given.

E. H. H.

The task was great and time was pressing, so the work was divided between Wycliffe and his friend Nicholas of Hereford. Wycliffe started on the Book of Revelation, then translated the Gospels, and worked on the other books of the New Testament.

Nicholas set to work on the Old Testament—but was never allowed to finish it. In the Bodleian Library at Oxford to-day his manuscript is preserved, and the translation breaks off suddenly in the middle of a chapter —for Nicholas had to lay down his pen and appear in London on a charge of heresy. Imprisonment, excommunication, and banishment was his portion, and never was the chapter completed by him—other hands finished his work. Meanwhile, the popularity and high position occupied by Wycliffe stood him in good stead. He escaped the fate of Nicholas, and was able to plod quietly on until the New Testament was completed in 1380.

The spirit in which these " heroes of the Book " did their work, may be seen from the preface of Richard Purvey, who revised the Wycliffe Bible eight years later :

" A translator hath great need to study well the sense, both before and after, and then also he hath need to live a clean life, and be full devout in his prayers, and have not his wits occupied with worldly things : that the Holy Spirit, author of all wisdom and cunning and truth, dress him for his work, and suffer him not to err."*

Wycliffe's work was only just beginning. In that dark age printing was unknown, very few people could read, and the mother-tongue itself was in a very fluid state. Up to that time the English language had been despised. The language of the Church was Latin, and bad Latin at that. The language of the government,

* The spelling here has been modernised ; note that some of the words (*e.g.,* " cunning ") have changed their meaning.

the barons, and the nobles was French, brought over by the Norman Conqueror. Yet no difficulty, however great, could turn Wycliffe from his purpose ; so we find this learned and popular Oxford lecturer gathering eager young students round him, who were set hard at work making copies of the books of this new English Bible. Catching the enthusiasm and devotion of their beloved master, they laboured night and day at their copying, with such success that hundreds of copies of the Bible, or parts of the Bible, were made and passed round. About 170 copies survive to this day, some of them beautifully written and illuminated for people of rank and wealth ; many are plain, neat copies for use by preachers and teachers ; some are small copies made to be carried in the pocket, or inexpensive copies of the Gospels and Psalms for people of small means.

Large sums of money were paid for even a few leaves of these hand-written Bibles. A load of hay was given for permission to read the Book for one hour per day during a short period. Many simple folk learned short passages by heart, and were in great demand for secret gatherings of people, who eagerly met in the heart of a wood, or other out-of-the-way place, to hear the Ten Commandments, or chapters from the Gospels or Epistles, recited. " So the Word of God grew and multiplied."

Wycliffe rejoiced to see the light of truth spreading more and more in his beloved land. But the work went on against fierce opposition of bishops, priests and monks ; ranged against Wycliffe were all the forces of the Church and the might of the Pope. At every opportunity copies of the English Bible or its parts were seized and destroyed, and their owners punished. Yet nothing could really stop the spreading of the light. In spite of all the bishops could do, the circulating and reading of the Bible went on.

The "Poor Preachers."

So great was the hunger for "Godde's lawe," as it was called, that Wycliffe was led to take a further step. Not only should the Bible be given to all who could afford a copy, but "the poor should have the Gospel preached unto them." This also sounds very ordinary to us, but in those dark days the good news of Christ was withheld from the people. Many of the clergy never went near their parishes, the churches were seldom open, and the services were read in Latin—an unknown tongue to the people.

Quietly Wycliffe arranged to alter all this; selecting the best of his students he prepared them for a great work. Like Jesus of old, he decided to send them out " two by two, without purse or scrip," to take the Gospel to the common people.

How many of these poor preachers Wycliffe sent out we know not, but we do know that their work has affected the whole course of English history. Clad in long russet gowns, carrying nothing but a staff and a copy of the English Bible, they tramped throughout the length and breadth of the land. They took no money with them, but they were never in want. On village green, outside humble cottages, in empty barns, in squire's hall or baron's castle, these poor preachers took their good news to the people of England, reading and teaching them from " Godde's lawe."

Wherever they went, they were received gladly by all classes of the people. No record has come down to us of any rules laid down by Wycliffe for their work ; their names and the number of them are unrecorded, but the work they did for religion and freedom will ever remain. Their russet gowns, their broad hats, their rolls of unbleached sheepskin, must have been a familiar sight throughout the English countryside.

The Pope and the bishops grew thoroughly alarmed

at the work of these poor preachers, but found that neither threats nor derision could stop their work. They dubbed them " Lollards," probably a term of derision from loller—a penniless and idle good-for-nothing, who spent his days lolling outside the village inn. Thus " Lollard " was a gibe at the poverty of Wycliffe's humble preachers, but the name soon became one of honour. The English people had had more than enough of wealthy and absentee clergy, or begging monks and friars, and gladly welcomed and listened to these poor preachers, who not only taught Christ's love but first followed it themselves.

Having given the people the English Bible, and sent them its good news by his poor preachers, Wycliffe devoted the rest of his life to improving his translation, and also to exposing the false teaching of the Pope. The time came when this King's chaplain and friend of princes fell into disfavour in high quarters, through his fearless teaching and his passion for spreading the light of religion among the masses of the people. His enemies watched for their opportunity to crush him.

Cast out of the Church.

Behold, then, another scene in London, this time in the great hall of the Black Friars' monastery, when monks and abbots, bishops and doctors assembled in purple robes and satin gowns for the trial of John Wycliffe. When the heretic enters and faces his judges, things are very different to that other trial in Old St. Paul's. Wycliffe is now an old man, and he stands alone. Earls and princes are no longer his protectors. While he was the champion of English liberty against a foreign Pope, he was a useful ally for prince and noble. But now that he has dared to attack the false teaching of the English Church he is allowed to be a prey for bishops and prelates.

In the simple black robe of the country rector, Wycliffe

stands forth in striking contrast to the fine linen and purple gowns of his judges. He faces them calm-eyed, fearless, and confident. Suddenly there is a cry of terror in the trial chamber. A loud rumbling fills the air, the building seems to rock on its foundation, friars and bishops grow pale with superstitious awe. On two previous occasions the trial of Wycliffe had been interrupted by a terrible storm. What did it mean ? Seeing the panic Archbishop Courtenay rises in his place.

" We shall not give up the trial," he thunders. " This earthquake but portends the purging of the kingdom. For as there are in the bowels of the earth noxious vapours, which only by a violent earthquake can be purged away, so are these evils brought by such men upon this land, which only by a very earthquake can be removed. Let the trial go forward."

As the charges are read it surprises us to find that " these evils " brought by Wycliffe, and needing " an earthquake to cleanse them away," included attacks on the evil lives of the clergy, exposing the system of indulgences as a fraud—" worst " of all, turning the sacred scriptures into the common tongue and giving them to the common people.

With leaders of the Church as judges, the result of this trial was a foregone conclusion. Wycliffe's teaching was condemned and he was excommunicated. Further than that they dare not go at that time. So condemned and despised, an outcast from the Church, Wycliffe went back to his vicarage at Lutterworth to work harder than ever at giving the Bible to the English people. Knowing the hatred and power of his enemies, he could not expect to be allowed to end his days in peace. But before the plans of his enemies could be completed against him the end came. On the last Sunday of 1384, as the brave old pioneer was conducting worship for his own people, he passed suddenly and peacefully away.

Like the Master he served, the reproach of his enemies became Wycliffe's greatest tribute. Here is their complaint against the Father of the English Bible :

" This master, John Wycliffe, translated the Gospel out of Latin into English, and by that means laid it more open to the laity and to women who could read than it used to be to the most learned of the clergy, and those of them who had the best understanding. And so the Gospel pearl is cast abroad and trodden under swine, and that which used to be precious to both clergy and laity is made as it were the common jests of both, and the jewel of the Church is turned into the sport of the laity."

NOTES ON THE YARN.

Aim.

To show how John Wycliffe proved a pioneer in giving the Gospel to the English people and translating the Bible into the English tongue.

Biographical.

The secret of Wycliffe's life and work was his acceptance of the Bible as the guide-book of life, powerful to reinforce a quickened conscience. Living in an age of spiritual darkness, and of spiritual wickedness in high places, his preaching and pioneer work would have been fruitless had his life not been in accord with the high moral standard he laid down for clergy and laity. Amid the hazy and incomplete records of his life one fact is clear—his worst enemies brought no charge against his personal character. William Thorpe, a disciple of Wycliffe, paid his master this high tribute : " Master John Wycliffe was considered by many to be the most holy of all the men in his age. He was of emaciated frame, spare, and well-nigh destitute of strength ; and he was absolutely blameless in his conduct. Wherefore, very many of the chief men in this kingdom, who frequently held counsel with him, were devotedly attached to him, kept a record of what he said, and guided themselves after his manner of life."

Wycliffe's birth is generally placed about 1325, and usually connected with the Manor of Wycliffe on the banks of the Tees near Richmond, Yorks. His parents must have had means, for he went to Oxford to complete his studies and soon became a popular teacher, at a time when this English University was second to none in Europe as a centre of light and learning. He became Master of Balliol College in 1360, but apparently resigned his Mastership on taking the college living at Fillingham. In 1374 he became Rector of Lutterworth, and held this living to the end. His crusade against papal errors and political claims of Rome brought him great honour and popularity. His denial of the right of the clergy to political power made him popular with John of Gaunt, Duke of Lancaster, who saved him from condemnation by the Bishop of London when cited to appear in St. Paul's, on February 19th, 1377 (as related in the beginning of the yarn). Proceeding with his campaign of "back to the Bible," he bent his energies for years to giving the Scriptures to the people in their own tongue, and in sending out his poor preachers to take the Gospel to the neglected masses. This daring enterprise could not have succeeded had it not been for the fact that the scandalous contest between the rival Popes at Rome and Avignon diverted attention from his work and saved him from martyrdom. When it was too late, the full power of the Church was launched against him and his work. Forty years after his death his bones were dug up and burnt, while the Lollards were destroyed by sword and fire, and to all appearances a reactionary Church had triumphed once more over a new spiritual movement. History proves, however, that the work of Wycliffe and his poor preachers acted as leaven in English life, and prepared the way for the movement on the Continent that blazed out later in the Reformation. Contrast with the testimony of his disciple, William Thorpe, quoted above, the following description of his death by his enemies : " John Wycliffe, the organ of the devil, the enemy of the Church, the idol of heretics, the image of hypocrites, the restorer of schism, the storehouse of lies, the sink of flattery, being struck by the horrible judgment of God, was seized by a palsy throughout his whole body, and that mouth which was to have spoken huge things against God and his saints and holy Church, was miserably drawn aside and afforded a frightful spectacle to beholders ; his tongue was speechless and his head shook, showing plainly that the curse which God had thundered forth against Cain was also inflicted on him." As a testimony to the scholarship and careful industry of Wycliffe, stands the fact that many fragments of his version of the Scriptures, although taken from the Latin vulgate (not from the original Greek or Hebrew), and at a time when the English language was in a fluid state, are almost identical with our authorised version of 1688. Hence the point of the famous words of Fuller concerning the ashes of Wycliffe, that were cast into the Swift hard by Lutterworth : " The Swift bore them into the Severn, and the Severn into the narrow seas, and they again into the ocean. Thus the ashes of Wycliffe are an emblem of his doctrines, which are dispersed over all the world."

Questions.

Why was the age of Wycliffe a time of spiritual darkness ?
How did he labour to "lighten the darkness" ?
Why is he called the Father of the English Bible ?
What did he accomplish through his Poor Preachers ?
What do we owe to him to-day ?

II

DOCTOR BARNARDO

Dates : B., 1845 *: D.,* 1905.

"To Heal the Broken-hearted"

The ragged school was over, and thoroughly tired out, the young medical student began to lock up for the night. He had started this ragged school in an empty stable, out of pity for the urchins of East London, in a dirty alley not far from the great London Hospital in Whitechapel Road, where he was training to be a doctor.

On this particular night one of the smaller ragamuffins crouched at the little stove, as though anxious to enjoy its warmth to the last possible moment. At last the student said :

" Come along now, you must go home."

" Let me stay 'ere, guv'nor," pleaded the boy. " My mate tole me as 'ow you might let me stay 'ere all night by the fire."

" Oh, no, run away home now," said the young medico.

" Got no home ! " said the boy quickly. " Don't live nowhere ; got no friends."

The student could hardly believe his ears, and scanned the boy's face keenly, still doubting and suspicious. But there was a hopeless and pinched look on the urchin's face that compelled him to put many more questions. Soon he was quite certain that the boy was not only homeless, but had not a friend in the world. Then the boy's eagerness to talk suddenly reawakened all his suspicions, and he felt certain he was being hoaxed ; for when he asked if there were any other homeless boys about, the urchin said :

" Oh, yes, sir ; lots—'eaps on 'em ; more'n I could count."

Almost angry at the barefaced way the boy was leading him on, young Barnardo determined to test the truth of this statement. He challenged the boy to show him these " lots " of homeless outcasts.

" Right you are, guv'nor ; foller me," said the boy, confidently.

The amazed student locked the old stable and hurried into the alley. A bitter wind was blowing, and he felt chilled to the bone, well wrapped up though he was. For the next quarter of an hour he followed his bare-footed and ragged guide through a wilderness of filthy alleys, to old sheds and tumble-down hovels, striking matches from time to time to peep under barrows or behind boxes and into dark corners. But nowhere was a boy to be seen !

" You said you could show me lots of them, and we can't find one," said Barnardo sharply.

" Stop a minit, and come arter me," said the urchin, and began to climb a wall like a rat. Reaching the top, he helped Barnardo to clamber up after him.

" Look there," said the boy triumphantly, with extended finger. In the pale light of the moon the student with horror counted eleven poor boys, sleeping in various positions in the gutter of the iron roof in front of him, with nothing to cover them but their ragged clothes.

" Shall I wake 'em up, sir ? " whispered the urchin.

" No, no," said the awestruck visitor, as he clambered down the wall.

" Shall I show you another lay, sir ; there's lots more ? "

But Barnardo had seen enough for one night. He took the boy to a lodging-house and provided him with food and a bed, then went slowly to his lodgings.

Dedicated to the Waifs.

The sight of those boys sleeping on the iron roof that bitter winter's night haunted young Barnardo for days. He must do something for those lads. He saw clearly what that midnight quest meant—beginning his life all over again ! He had purposed in his heart to devote his life to work for Jesus Christ in China, and had come to London to get medical training for missionary work. And lo, a great door of service had suddenly swung open in the heart of Christian England. With regret, but without faltering, he threw aside all his plans and dedicated his life to the service of Jesus Christ among the flotsam and jetsam of civilisation at home. He could do no other !

The way speedily opened for the beginning of this new work. A few evenings later young Barnardo sat among the great congregation that gathered every Sunday evening in the Agricultural Hall at Islington. Dr. Thane Davidson was holding Sunday Services for the People, but this night the man advertised to speak failed to appear. Recognising Barnardo in the audience, Dr. Davidson called him to the platform and announced :

" Our young friend here, a medical student, who is working in the East End among the street boys, will give an account of his mission."

With a quickly-beating heart the " young friend " nervously faced that great crowd. He had never spoken in public before, and hardly knew how to begin. With a momentary prayer to God for help, young Barnardo braced himself for the ordeal, fighting down his nervousness, for this was his hour of opportunity.

Very simply he began to tell the people the story of
the urchin who would not go home, and of the quest
that followed in the purlieus of East London. Amid a
silence that could be felt, the vast audience hung upon
his words, deeply moved by his plain tale.

When the meeting broke up a young servant girl
nervously approached him and pressed a small package
into his hand. " This is all I can afford from my small
earnings," she said ; " I have saved it as a gift for
foreign missions, but I want you to have it for your
work."

The young medico stammered his thanks, and felt
more embarrassed than the girl.

" This was the first public money I ever received," he
said afterwards. " I felt myself getting red and hot all
over. The question rose in my mind, ' Could I take it,
was it right ? ' It seemed ungracious to refuse the gift,
so I held the little parcel in my hand and thanked her
in some awkward fashion. I know I felt as awkward
in receiving it as she did in giving it. When at last
I reached home I opened the packet, and found it con-
tained 6$\frac{3}{4}$d. in farthings. I knew not what to do, nor
what to think in regard to the gift. Presently, however,
it came home to me that I had been asking God for
guidance and help, and that this was His way of giving
both."

An account of that meeting appeared in the newspapers
next day, and caught the eye of the great Earl of
Shaftesbury, then hard at work on behalf of the child
toilers of the land. To the utter surprise of Barnardo,
the postman brought him an invitation to dine with
the Earl at his West-end home. At the Earl's dining-
table he met a number of high-born gentlemen, to whom
he repeated the story of his midnight quest ; but as
he did so Barnardo saw plainly that they thought he
was painting a picture from his imagination. At once

the Earl came to his rescue ; it was a simple matter to test his story.

" Can you take us to places where children can actually be seen sleeping under the open sky this bitter night ? "

" I can," replied Barnardo, without a moment's hesitation.

That night a strange sight was seen in some of the filthiest slums in East London, as a party of gentlemen in evening dress were piloted by young Barnardo on a tour of inspection. But not a boy could be discovered anywhere. Some of the gentlemen began to wear an " I told you so " air, the Earl looked surprised, and Barnardo felt very vexed, but would not give up. Explaining his quest to a friendly policeman, the constable pointed into the blackness of a yard, saying :

" It's all right ; there's a lot of 'em in there. They will come out if you give them a copper."

Stepping into the evil-smelling blackness, Barnardo offered a halfpenny a head to any boys there. The result was staggering. Out of a pile of old crates, boxes, and empty barrels there slowly crawled seventy-three boys.

" There they stood beneath the light of a lamp, a sorrowful regiment of the great army of the destitute, lined up before an even more sorrowful regiment of the well-to-do," said Dr. Barnardo afterwards. " I pray God that I may never again behold such a sight. As my visitors insisted on feeding the boys, I told them I knew a coffee-shop open all night. So thither we all trooped, and our company carried the place by storm, and filled it right out twice over. Moreover, the shopkeeper supplied change for half-a-sovereign in coppers, for the promised halfpenny to each boy."

The Beginning of the Enterprise.

The disused donkey's stable rapidly became not only a ragged school, but a home for destitute waifs—work that claimed so many days and nights of Barnardo's time that his medical studies were sadly neglected. Lord Shaftesbury and others strongly urged young Barnardo to devote his life to the cause of the waif children. For a moment he hesitated, for if he took the plunge he knew that hundreds of destitute children would swarm around him in need of help, and where would the money come from ? At that moment he had nearly twenty boys on his hands, provided for in various lodgings by the gifts of a few friends. Soberly the young student sat down to face up to the future. If the number of these children were increased, what could he do with them ? He would need some kind of a home to put them into. They would need education and training, as well as food and clothing, and a roof over their heads. Their future would have to be carefully thought of and provided for. Would not the burden prove too great ?

More than ever in his life before he prayed to God for guidance. One day the answer came. The words : " I will guide thee with mine eye " seemed written in letters of fire in the Bible before him, and fastened themselves upon his mind in such a way that he felt that here was all he wanted. The question was settled once and for all ! With all his fears quieted, with peace of mind, and heart at rest, Barnardo gave himself entirely to the service of the waifs.

In Stepney Causeway he opened his first Home for Destitute Children. It was a tremendous venture of faith, for he at once became the foster-father to a family that steadily increased in number daily. From the start he determined to have " an ever-open door," and that no destitute child should ever be refused admittance. He had no wealth of his own to keep his ever-growing family, but he could pray that God would provide for their needs.

That the doctor was made of heroic stuff is plain from the bold lines upon which his work was started. Steadily he set his face against half-measures that would save money but spoil his work. Others have followed along the road that he blazed out, but he was the pioneer in this work. Alert to the drawbacks of herding great numbers of poor children together in barrack-like places, or branding them as objects of charity by putting them into a uniform, he made the bold experiment of " boarding out " his children, and so giving them the blessings of home life.

He was the first to start labour houses, where older boys could learn useful trades and be helped to become useful citizens. He was the first to see the wisdom of mixing up his crippled children with those who were sound and healthy ; for he was quick to realise that to put a cripple into a houseful of cripples would condemn them all to a life of misery, and rob sound children of the opportunity of helping the less-favoured ones.

The Ever-open Door.

Like a rolling snowball Dr. Barnardo's Home grew bigger and bigger, and his ever-increasing family became spread farther and farther afield. His work made greater demands than ever upon his time and strength, and the problem of paying his household expenses assumed alarming proportions. To get money for this he toured the country, sometimes seeing very little result for his efforts. Yet never was he left in despair. When the need was greatest he simply went down on his knees and told his Heavenly Father all about it, and never once did his faith prove in vain.

One winter a very severe spell of cold weather found his many children shivering in their beds, for there were no warm blankets, and no money to buy them. His prayers seemed unheard, for no money came in. In

strong faith the doctor went next morning to a ware-
house to select the blankets he would need, and find
out their cost. He came away without placing the order,
for he would need £100 to meet it, and he always refused
to go into debt. Next morning a clergyman in the
South of England, quite unknown to him, sent a cheque
for £100 " to pay the cost of additional warm clothing
that you must need during this cold weather." The
doctor was not long in placing his order for blankets !

Sometimes the doctor spent his last shilling, but never
have his thousands of children been sent supperless to
bed—the money always came because their foster-father
always prayed in faith for it.

As more and more destitute children filed through that
" ever-open door " in Stepney Causeway, the work of the
benevolent doctor grew heavier and heavier. New
buildings were constantly required to provide shelter,
schooling, or work for his large family.

As the years passed all sorts of people, of all ages,
sent gifts for his treasury—the rich with their bank-
notes, and the poor with their widows' mites.

One night at a big meeting far from London, a little
girl of seven, poorly clad, shyly sidled up to the doctor
and gave him sixpence, whispering :

" That's for your poor little gells," then adding in a
trembling whisper, " May I kiss you ? "

Like all pioneers, Barnardo was often denounced as a
crank, a dreamer and a madman, when launching out on
new and untried lines. The truth is, he had great
ambitions for his family of unfortunate children. To him
they were not mere objects of charity. His great heart
was big enough to love them all as though they were his
own children, and he planned to give them all a real
home.

For his girls he wanted cottage homes in the country,
where they could live in little family groups, instead of

being herded together in a dreary, barrack-like building in East London. When he talked of this, and wrote to the newspapers about it, the idea was scoffed at by many as a madman's freak. This did not worry the doctor, who waited for Divine guidance. It came! One day he went down to Oxford for a meeting on behalf of his work, and stayed the night in an hotel there. Next morning a stranger spoke to him.

" I noticed your name in the visitors' list, Dr. Barnardo," said the man, " and I've been reading about your plan of country cottages, and a village home for girls. Put me down for the first cottage ! "

That was the beginning of the Girls' Village Home near Ilford, where amid delightful surroundings cottages are grouped round the village green, with a church and schools where the girl waifs of our great cities can grow up into healthy and useful women.

The day came when the doctor had another plan. Through that " ever-open door " destitute and unwanted babies were often brought by older brothers and sisters, or by the scouts sent out by the doctor on expeditions of mercy—once a baby was delivered by Carter Patersons' in a box !

How could the tender-hearted doctor refuse babies, yet what could he do with them all ? If only he had a big house in the country, that could be made into a nursery for them. The plan grew in his mind, and he prayed and waited. And one day he received the gift of a big house at Hawkhurst, in the midst of the Kentish meadows. Here was the answer to his prayer. He put thirty babies in the house with their nurses, and called it " Babies' Castle."

The Other Door.

Before his work had been going on very long the doctor discovered that he would need two doors, not one.

A door that ever opened inwards to receive destitute children meant that before long there must be another door opening outwards, through which grown-up members could pass out to take their place in the world. This " ever-open exit " brought its own cares and problems, but the pioneer was never at a loss for a plan. He saw clearly that his work had largely failed if his children passed out into the world untrained, and left to shift for themselves. So he set himself the task of passing out well-trained youths and girls, who could earn their own living and become useful members of the community. This meant that training-homes and workshops must be started where skilled trades could be taught. It also meant keeping in touch with those who passed out, so that they would not be left alone in the world.

In the cry of the British Colonies for men, Dr. Barnardo was the first to hear a call to new careers for grown-up members of his family. Thus began the Immigration Department of the Homes—the first of its kind—by which thousands of street arabs and gutter-snipes of the old country have become prosperous settlers in our overseas dominions.

In the demand for men for the British Navy and Mercantile Marine, the doctor saw another great opportunity for his grown-up boys. The spell that the sea has ever cast over the boys of England made it easy for him to draft large numbers of the older boys into the Navy. Before long this brought him face to face with the problem of getting a training ship, to prepare these boys for a life on the ocean wave. For this training ship he prayed and waited year after year, but it did not come. At last, through the generosity of Mr. E. H. Watts and his son, he was able to buy a disused school in Norfolk, near the coast, and start the Watts' Naval Training School. With the help of these and other friends the interior of the great building was made as much like a ship as possible. When the "crew" is full there are 350 boys "on board this ship on the land," and naval training there is complete. Even time is kept by ship's bells and not by a clock. After their training on this land ship, the boys are drafted to a real training ship off the neighbouring coast, so that they can pass into the Navy or the Mercantile Marine fully trained for a sailor's life.

Dr. Barnardo has now passed on to higher service, but his work goes on. The truth is that a man with his spirit cannot die, but lives on in the hearts and lives of the men and women who keep his work going. To-day the great institution he started still keeps its "ever-open door."

NOTES ON THE YARN

Aim.

To show how Dr. Barnardo devoted his life to the destitute and suffering children of Britain, and became a pioneer in rescue and waif work.

Historical.

Although not yet eighty years old, the Institution founded by Dr. Barnardo has secured a permanent place in Christian philanthropy through the devotion, statesmanship, energy and sound judgment of its founder. Dr. Barnardo was in many directions a man of genius, and his life-story is a remarkable example of what one man can do when his life is dedicated to Christ and his energies harnessed for the good of humanity. One of his intimate workers wrote : "As I picture him to myself to-day, he seems to me to have had the face of a doctor, the eyes of a lawyer, the figure of a Napoleon, the head of a banker, the tongue of an orator, and the heart of a Christian . . . he was a man, every inch of him—a man of energy, decision, resource, command, independence, insight, vivid imagination, analytical mind, and wide but pure ambition, whose magnetism thrilled men and women of all ranks and classes, whose humour well balanced his pathos ; a man of prayer, a man of faith—a man of God." Because he had high ideals, he set an unusually high standard in Christian service. Enthusiastic and thorough in his methods, he had a profound belief in the worth and importance of the child. To understand this last point is to realise why Barnardo became a pioneer of new methods among ragged and destitute children. He founded his work on the principle that charity should be as warm-blooded and tender-hearted towards her children as the best of parents. To realise this is to appreciate why Barnardo would have nothing whatever to do with the dreary barrack-room and pauper uniform of the Poor Law child. It explains, too, the large-hearted faith of the founder of a charity that grew to include a girls' model village, a boys' garden city, thousands of boarded-out children and an immigration farm.

Biographical.

Thomas John Barnardo was born in Dublin in 1845, his father being Spanish and his mother English. He was endowed with a wiry physical frame, with great mental energy, with the quick temper and passionate determination associated with Ireland, and an intensity of spiritual character that led him to devote his life early to the service of Jesus Christ. An ardent Protestant and a fervent evangelical, he chose a medical missionary career and came to England in 1866 as a medical student attached to the London Hospital in the East End. He lodged within 200 yards of a slum known as Stepney Causeway, and from the outset gained a first-hand knowledge of the tragedy of slum life. In 1867 he took a house at 18, Stepney Causeway, and here "Dr. Barnardo's Homes" formally began operations with twenty-five boys in residence. "It had no capital," wrote Dr. Barnardo afterwards, "and was opened in defiance of all the rules of worldly prudence." Dr. Barnardo's schemes were always ahead of his resources, for the simple reason that the field of opportunity was practically limitless. By 1873 he found himself free to develop his work on systematic lines—he also completed his medical studies and took his F.R.C.S. Ed. degree, married a wife, and made his home at Barkingside. Later came a period of storm, criticism and attack. The law was then on the side of the parent, and it was invoked against the charitable work of the doctor. Twelve cases were brought against him, but nine resulted in his favour, and of the other three public opinion saw that he was morally right, though technically on the wrong side of the law. These attacks, however, served a very great purpose, for as the result of them the law was amended to protect the child from unnatural parents. As the years passed Dr. Barnardo's family increased rapidly, and his methods were copied by other organisations. Taking the widest possible view of his responsibilities as a foster-parent, the doctor shouldered the immense task of training his children to become useful citizens. In 1893 the doctor's heart literally began to break down under the strain of his full life, and for twelve years he fought a battle against heart disease. Up to the last he remained the busiest man in London, and died suddenly, "in harness," on 19th September, 1905.

To estimate rightly the work accomplished by Dr. Barnardo, and still being carried on on the principles laid down by him, the last report should be secured from the Secretary, 18/26, Stepney Causeway, E. 1. There are over 7,000 boys and girls being cared for, about half of them being boarded out in country homes.

Questions:

Do you think Dr. Barnardo was justified in giving up a career as a medical missionary ?

How did he prove himself a pioneer ?

What points in his character made him successful in his work ?

Discuss plans for helping on his work.

III

ELIZABETH FRY

(*Dates : B.*, 1780 *: D.*, 1845)

"DELIVERANCE TO THE CAPTIVES"

The driver of the old stage coach lashed his horses to a furious gallop. He was behind time, and would be late in arriving at Norwich, so with a clear stretch of country road before him, he tried to put on speed. Suddenly a bevy of girls some way ahead spread themselves right across the road and, linking arms, waited for the oncoming coach. In vain the postilion blew his horn and the driver shouted. Giggling with impudence, the seven sisters refused to budge and the coach had to be brought to a standstill. Having succeeded in their mischief, the girls ran off in great glee.

Had their father seen this prank he would have been deeply grieved, for far and wide people respected John Gurney, the Quaker banker of Norwich. His large family were in the care of Kitty, the eldest girl, who at seventeen had to become mother to six sisters and five brothers. In spite of their Quaker heritage, the children were usually ready for mischief, high-spirited, fond of music and dancing and society. Among the girls Elizabeth was the gentlest and most retiring, but she was voted obstinate by her sisters.

On Sundays (First Day, they called it) John Gurney escorted his children to the Quaker Meeting House in Goat Lane. The quiet and sober worship of the Meeting

House was not altogether to the liking of the girls, for they often returned home " goatified," as they called it, and happy to escape from Goat's.

One Sunday the seven sisters sat in a row as usual under the gallery, but on this occasion seemed much more interested than usual. Even Elizabeth forgot to be restless, and stopped admiring the very smart pair of purple new boots, laced with scarlet that she was wearing. On this occasion William Savery, an American Quaker, was preaching, and in a voice and manner that could not fail to arrest attention. Long before the sermon was ended Elizabeth was deeply moved, and the tears were streaming down her cheeks. The fact is Elizabeth's religious nature was on the eve of a great development. Next morning William Savery called at their house to have a long talk with Elizabeth, and at its close he foretold that she would become a preacher and spend her days in noble service.

" From that day her love of pleasure and of the world seemed gone," wrote one of the sisters afterwards. Among the good resolutions she entered in her diary at this time was the vow " not to be vain or silly ; to be independent of the opinion of others ; not to make dress a study, and to read the Bible at all opportunities." Next she made the strange request that her father should take her to London, that she might see for herself the gay life of the great city. With sound common-sense Joseph Gurney agreed to this plan, desiring that his daughter should see something of the world before renouncing it for a religious life.

So for several weeks Elizabeth plunged into the gay life of London, going to theatres, attending balls, making the acquaintance of leading actresses, mixing in high society, and even seeing the Prince of Wales at an opera. She also saw a great deal of William Savery and other leading Quakers.

Before she left London she had a strange experience that helped her to this decision. At a meeting of London Quakers an old lady arose and pointing to the young girl with her bright and eager face, said slowly :

" Thou shalt be a light to the blind, speech to the dumb, and feet to the lame."

Deeply moved and surprised, Elizabeth said under her breath : " Can this be ? "

Then she went back home to think over all she had seen and heard. She found there was no real joy or lasting satisfaction in the amusements and vanity of the world, so solemnly renounced them and dedicated her life to the service of God and the good of others. No more purple boots and gay apparel for her ; in spite of her sisters' teasing, she adopted the grey gown and poke bonnet of the strict Quaker.

First Visit to Newgate.

By the time that she was twenty-eight the prophecy of William Savery came true, for after much hesitation she became a recognised minister, appointed to preach after the fashion of the Quakers. By this time she was married, and in spite of the cares of a large family, visited the sick and helped the poor in the villages around. " Madame Fry," as she was called, taught the poor children in a school she had started for them, distributed garments and Bibles among their parents, vaccinated the babies when smallpox threatened, and was ready to help every need.

One day, as her husband came home, he saw their one and only cow being led out into the village. Upon enquiry he learned that his wife was lending the animal to a poor woman who wanted extra milk for sale. " My dear, what will we lend next ? " he exclaimed.

One day two Friends called to tell her their story of a visit to Newgate Prison, and as she listened she was moved to tears, and almost before they had called for her help, she promised it.

The next morning found Elizabeth and another woman at the gate of Newgate Prison, with an urgent request to see the governor. Without waste of words, she asked to be shown the women's wards, but the governor begged her to give up all idea of it.

" The women are so wild and ferocious," he declared, " that, although soldiers are posted on duty, I myself never enter that part of the prison, if I can avoid it."

Nothing that he could say, however, would turn Elizabeth from her purpose, so before admitting them he begged them to leave their watches in his care, for they would assuredly be snatched away by the lawless women inside. But Elizabeth was neither fearful nor half-hearted in her work of mercy, and she refused ; so calling a turnkey the governor led them to the female wards.

The impression left by what she saw that morning remained with Elizabeth Fry throughout her life. She found about 300 women and numberless children crowded together in two small wards, in the custody of an old man and his son. They cooked, lived, and slept on the floor. If a stranger appeared they clamoured for money, with which they bought alcoholic drink from a bar in the prison. As Elizabeth faced these women it demanded all her courage not to shrink from the terrible noise, the filth, the horrible smells, and the perils of gaol fever. She could well believe the stories the governor had told her of the wild screaming, the bad language, and the constant fighting that went on there.

Yet what could she do ? To remedy this terrible state of affairs would demand the prolonged labour of a Hercules, whereas she was in poor health, and had many boys and girls of her own at home to care for ! She spoke kindly to the women, to their utter astonishment ;

and seeing that her words had impressed them, she knelt down to pray for them. She was surprised to find that most of the women knelt too, and when the prayer was over many were in tears. Finally, she promised to send some clothes for those who were but partially covered.

Working through the Child.

Three years passed, but Elizabeth Fry had not forgotten the women of Newgate, in spite of trouble and death among her own children. Carefully she had been preparing her plans, and in 1817 came to London, leaving her children in her sister's care. The labour of Hercules was to be tackled in a very thorough manner. This time she faced the three hundred women alone, and, to the horror of the jailer, begged to be shut in alone with them.

" The railing was crowded with half-naked women, struggling together for the front places with the most boisterous violence, and begging with the utmost noise. I felt as if I were going into a den of wild beasts, and can still recollect shuddering when the door was closed upon me and I was locked in with such a herd of novel and desperate companions," she said years afterwards.

She read them one of the Gospel parables, and noticing that even in such a terrible plight they still cared for their children, began her scheme of help by promising to start a school, so that the little ones should have a better chance in life than they had had.

The women hailed the idea with tears of joy. On her next visit they had chosen their teacher in Mary Connor, a young woman who had had a smattering of education, and was in prison for stealing a watch. On her part Elizabeth Fry had not been idle. She had explained her scheme for a prison school to the governor, and to the sheriffs of London, and though at first they had scoffed at the very idea of it, in the end they pledged themselves to back her up. They gave her the use of an unoccupied cell as a schoolroom, and the Newgate School started in earnest. With help, Mary Connor became quite a good teacher, and the miserable lot of the prison children became greatly improved.

Every day Elizabeth Fry went in and out of the prison with her friends to help in the school, and she soon felt that something must be done for the mothers. Apart from the lack of food, the terrible overcrowding and the dirt, the women had nothing to occupy their hands or minds, so that the days were spent in begging, swearing, gaming, fighting, dancing, dressing up in men's clothes, and in scenes too bad to be described. Under her leadership a committee of ladies was formed to help the women prisoners, and for a month they gave their whole time " to provide for the clothing, instruction and employment of the women, to teach them the Bible, and to form in them habits of sobriety, order and industry."

This plan, drawn up by Elizabeth Fry, reveals her pioneer spirit ; she was the first to see what everyone accepts now, that a prison should reform and help the prisoner to a better life. She bent all her energies, therefore, to change completely the prison system of England. So long as women were herded together and tortured in this way, they would be hardened, brutalised and made revengeful. Her bold plan was to change all that, and secure that their time in prison should help the women to make a fresh start in life after their release By dint of hard work she persuaded the prison authorities to lend their aid for her scheme.

One Sunday afternoon a remarkable scene occurred— for the first time the women prisoners were amazed to see their champion and her women friends usher into the filthy cell the sheriffs and high officials of the prison.

Speaking simply and quietly, Elizabeth explained to the women her plans for helping them, making it very clear that their help and willingness was essential. She then put before them a set of rules that they must accept and loyally carry out. These rules provided that there was to be no more begging, swearing, gaming or quarrelling ; that the prisoners should be formed into classes, that they should appoint monitors for these classes, and that needlework, knitting, and other suitable work should be undertaken. To the surprise of the officials, every woman raised her hand in assent when these rules were voted upon. Believing that the prisoners would " play the game," Elizabeth Fry secured a disused laundry for a workroom, raised money to get materials, and set the women to work under the monitors they had themselves chosen.

The Prison as School.

After giving the school a month's trial, it was voted a tremendous success by Elizabeth Fry and all her workers, so she determined the time was ripe for her next move. She invited the Lord Mayor of London and other authorities to inspect the school, and to see for themselves the enormous change that had taken place in one month in the women. The visitors were amazed and delighted, for what had been called hitherto a " hell upon earth " was now a scene of industry, order and quiet. They could hardly believe their eyes, when, instead of the half-clothed mob of screaming, fighting women, they saw a company of neatly-dressed prisoners, working quietly and obeying the orders of their monitors. The city authorities withdrew, and later passed a vote of congratulation and thanks to Elizabeth Fry and her friends for the wonderful work they had done.

This was just what Elizabeth wanted—not the thanks, but the recognition of the good work done, for it gave her the chance to urge that her scheme to improve the lot of prisoners should be taken over by the authorities, and made part and parcel of the prison system. She demanded more room, to end the overcrowding, the appointment of women officials for the women's prison, a proper allowance of food and clothing, and work provided for them, that the system of classes and monitors should be continued, and religious instruction regularly given. These demands were not all acceded to at the time, but as a direct result of this pioneer work they became in time part of the prison system of the land.

Part of the horrors of prison life at that time was the custom of transportation, *i.e.*, shipping prisoners to convict settlements in distant Colonies. Elizabeth Fry came up against this evil, for almost on her first visit to Newgate the turnkey related to her, almost with trembling, the terrible scenes in the women's prison on the night before a party for Botany Bay were to start. To celebrate the parting with their fellow prisoners, and to give them a good send-off, it was the custom for the women to pull down and break everything they could lay their hands on, and to spend the night in violence and drunkenness. On the following morning they would be taken to the docks, in open carts through the streets, to be jeered at by the public and cheered by their friends.

On Convict Ships.

Here was work in abundance for our pioneer, and she accepted the challenge with a right good will. The time came when the next party for Botany Bay was due to leave the prison, now so completely changed through Elizabeth Fry's labours. She prepared her plans, talked to the distressed women of the party and promised them her help. To the utter amazement of the turnkey, no noise was heard in the large cell and not a window was

broken. Next morning the party bade a quiet farewell
to the other prisoners and got into closed cabs that
Elizabeth Fry had persuaded the governor to use instead
of the open carts. Faithful to her promise, Elizabeth
and some friends went with the women to the docks.
On this occasion there was no riot and no street scenes.
When the ship was reached further wonders were wit-
nessed, for the women went quietly on board and settled
down peacefully in readiness for the voyage. During
the weeks that passed before the ship sailed, Elizabeth
regularly visited the women, and with her help the system
of monitors and useful work took the place of the idleness
and riotous conduct that had hitherto marked the
voyage.

This side of her work proved a heavy burden, and at
times a real peril. For twenty-three years she visited
every transport which sailed with prisoners from England. Often these journeys had to be made when she
was in bad health, and at the worst times of the year.

One day during a storm the harbour master at
Ramsgate saw a small boat labouring against the gale,
hardly making any progress, tossed on the waves like a
cork, and in danger of being swamped altogether. Going
out in his tug to its assistance, he found the passengers
were two ladies in Quaker garb, drenched to the skin
with the heavy storm and the spume of the sea. With
great difficulty the boat was secured by a rope and the
ladies helped on board.

One of the ladies thanked the captain in what he
afterwards termed " a dignified but beautiful expression."

" It is kind of thee, captain ; we thank thee. We
made no sign to thee ; having held up our handkerchiefs
to the other steamers, we did not think we would succeed
with thee."

It was Elizabeth Fry, who had been visiting a convict
ship.

No part of her prison work caused Elizabeth Fry so much heartache as the help she gave to condemned prisoners under sentence of death. The English law at this time seemed to hold life cheaper than property, and the death sentence was passed on men, women and even children for trivial offences. Scores of prisoners were sentenced to death every month. In one case a boy of nine, who poked a stick through a pane of glass in a shop window and stole some paints worth twopence, was sentenced to death for the offence. On such occasions Elizabeth Fry worked herself almost to exhaustion and frenzy in trying to get the sentence altered. As in the case of other reforms, she was not satisfied with success in saving individual lives, but gave the authorities no rest until the penal laws had been reformed, and the death sentence was only applied to the taking of human life.

To the end of her long life Elizabeth Fry devoted herself to the service of others. Despite weakness of health she travelled over many parts of Europe, visiting prisons and helping to secure the same reforms that she had won in her own country.

NOTES ON THE YARN

Aim.

To show how Elizabeth Fry became a pioneer of prison reform, through the consecration of her talents to the service of Jesus Christ.

Biographical.

The life of Elizabeth Fry is a remarkable example of the service that can be rendered by a strong will and a winsome personality, consecrated to the highest service. This pioneer of prison reform fought all her battles handicapped with weak health and the care of a large family. She also had the handicap of her sex, living at a time when a woman's life was circumscribed within very narrow limits by the public opinion and conventions of her day. Brought up in a Christian home, her religious nature blossomed to an unusual state of perfection in the congenial spiritual atmosphere of the Society of Friends. As a child she was very obstinate, but she schooled this until it became the driving power that made her persevere firmly in her mission, and she overcame her timidity until both physical and moral courage were developed. That penetrating critic, Thomas Carlyle, hearing her read the Bible in Newgate " with those silvery tones of hers," declared that she was "looking like a little spot of purity in a great sweltering mass of corruption." Wherever she went, her state-liness and charm made her the cynosure of all eyes. A pen portrait of the time describes her thus : " She is both lovely and wonderful on close acquaintance ; such energy, combined with meekness, and so much power with entire teachableness, are rarely found."

Elizabeth Fry was born on May 21st, 1780, third daughter of John Gurney, of Earlham Hall, Norwich, a Quaker banker. She was so mild-mannered and retiring, that it was not recognised that she was the most gifted of a family of eleven well-endowed children. At eighteen she had a religious experience that led her to become a " Plain Friend," *i.e.*, a Quaker of the stricter sort. From the outset her religion took a practical turn, as will be seen from the yarn. Her zeal for religious and philanthropic work made her hold back from marriage for a long time, but she ultimately married Joseph Fry. In 1810 she became a preacher among the Friends, and in 1813 visited Newgate for the first time. Although profoundly moved by the plight of the women prisoners, she was unable to do much to help them until 1817, when her real life-work began. In addition to the care of her eleven children, several of whom were born after her prison work had got into its full stride, she laboured hard to educate public opinion on the general question of prison reform, thus introducing a new era of British justice. Having mixed in good society in early life, she was able to win the support of leading men in both Houses of Parliament, and also gain the ear of royalty for her reforms. She not only visited prisons in all parts of England and Scotland, but travelled on the Continent in pur-suance of her life-work. Her influence even spread to the Antipodes, for she did much to improve the condition of female convicts transported to Southern Seas. In a real sense she is the mother of penal reform, for the methods she introduced for lessening the horrors of prison life and setting the prisoners to useful work, contain the germ of the modern system that aims at making the punishment of crime a remedial and not a vindictive measure. She lived long enough to see her work bearing fruit all over Europe; she died at Ramsgate on October 12th, 1845.

Towards the close of the seventeenth century the Society for the Promotion of Christian Knowledge had began investigating the condition of English prisons, but no reform came till towards the end of the eighteenth century when John Howard (B., 1726 ; D., 1790) devoted his life, and became a martyr to, prison reform. Howard worked hard and was partly successful in getting some of the worst horrors of life in prisons abolished, dying from typhus fever during his investigation of prison conditions in Russia. He described himself as " the plodder who goes about to collect materials for men of genius to make use of." Subsequent history showed that his work had little permanent result until this woman of genius took it up, and so developed it as to warrant her title of pioneer.

Questions.

What do you think was the motive power that drove Elizabeth Fry to take up her work for prisoners ?

In what way did she prove herself a pioneer in prison reform ?

Discuss the highest aim in punishing crime, and the best methods of carrying it out.

IV

LOUIS BRAILLE

Dates : B., 1809 : D., 1852.

FRANCIS JOSEPH CAMPBELL

Dates : B., 1834 : D., 1914.

" SIGHT TO THE BLIND."

In a harness maker's shop in Paris, just over 100 years ago, a small boy of three was playing at " copying father." Often he had watched his father cut the stout leather in long strips with his sharp knife, and had admired the strength that drove the long, sharp awl through the hard leather. He, too, wanted to make harness; as the sharp knife was kept out of reach, the boy seized an awl and, picking up a piece of waste leather, tried to bore a hole as he had seen his father do.

The leather was hard, and the boy had not much strength ; but he was a determined little chap, and pressed on the awl with all his might. Suddenly the leather slipped, the awl flew upwards and, alas! its sharp point entered his eye. His screams brought his father and mother into the shop. They ran with him to a doctor's, but one glance at the wounded eye showed the doctor that the sight was destroyed. In a short space of time his other eye grew inflamed in sympathy, and in a few months the poor lad was totally blind.

The next few years were sad ones for little Louis Braille, living in the darkness. The hope that sustained him was his father's promise that as soon as he was old enough he should go to the school for the blind. At last the day came when he entered the Blind School in Paris, and his days of idleness and dreary monotony were over. He proved a keen and clever scholar, and soon could read easily the raised letters that were used at that time in books for the blind. It soon became clear, too, that he had musical talent.

By the time he was fifteen, Louis was such a brilliant musician that he easily secured a post as organist in one of the Paris churches. He also made such strides with mathematics, geography, algebra, and other subjects that he was appointed a professor at the school he had entered seven years earlier as a pupil. His future was now assured, and his parents and friends saw a brilliant and successful career opening out for the harness maker's blind son.

An Accident Turned to Good Account.

By this time, however, Louis Braille had nobler ambitions than to become a successful professor or a brilliant organist. As a humble follower of Jesus Christ, his ruling passion was to use his gifts, not for his own advancement, but in the service of others. His school work impressed him with the need for a simpler method of teaching the blind to read. Few of his blind pupils had his gift for learning, and only by very slow degrees were they able to learn to read the raised letters in the clumsy books then in use.

Patiently Braille set to work to discover a simpler form of blind-writing and reading. Now he turned to good account the dangerous "playing with edged tools" that in his childhood had cost him his sight. He remembered that when unable to drive an awl right through the leather the point of the tool had raised a dot on the other side of the strap. This set him thinking, with the result that he once more took up awl and leather, not for play but for serious purpose. Hour after hour he punched holes half-way through the leather, making curious groups of dots on its underside. In this way he invented little groups of dots to represent the alphabet, then combinations of dots that would make syllables and short words. So, by slow degrees, he invented a " blind language " that enabled his pupils to write quickly and easily.

His dot system was so superior to the old raised-letter alphabet that when Braille explained his method to the public it created quite a sensation. He was only twenty at this time, and the system was far from perfect, but men everywhere recognised that this brilliant young blind professor had conferred an immense boon upon his fellow-blind. Encouraged by the success of these first experiments Braille continued to devote his time and strength to improving his system and adapting it for music, so as to make it of still greater service.

From the age of twenty-six he was in the grip of consumption, yet not for one minute would he cease his work as a teacher of the blind. Gentle in manner, kind in thought, he became the friend, guide and counsellor of all his pupils.

A story told of him reveals that Braille was a Greatheart. One of his pupils, who was leaving the institution, was unable to find work, and had no means of a livelihood. Discovering the truth, Braille resigned the position of organist he was then holding, in order that his pupil might step into the post and so be saved from destitution. That act was typical of the man.

When Louis Braille died at the early age of forty-three, hundreds of blind people mourned his loss as that of a very dear friend. The system he invented has been an untold blessing to the blind ever since, and although others have been tried the Braille method still holds the field.

*   *   *   *   *

When the Stars Faded.

A few years after Braille, in Paris, gave his system of blind-writing to the world, a boy was born in Tennessee, United States, who was destined to become another great benefactor of the blind. Francis Joseph Campbell, like Braille, had the great misfortune to lose his sight when about three years of age. He was playing one day on his father's farm when the long, sharp thorn of an acacia ran into his eye. Many anxious weeks followed, but despite all that could be done, the world became darker and darker for little Francis every day. The tragedy of those few weeks never faded from the boy's memory. Looking back after years of blindness he tells us :

" As my sight faded, my mother took me out every night before putting me to bed, and made me look up at the stars from the verandah. Little by little the curtain was drawn down ; one night I could see nothing.

" ' Why is it so dark ?   Why does not God light up the stars for your little boy ? '

" I remember to this day the tears which fell on my face as she carried me up to bed that night."

From that time onwards the gorgeous splendour of the summer in that Southern State remained only as a tender memory. The boy's parents were poor, the chances for education for the blind in Tennessee were few and very expensive, and it seemed as though Francis Campbell was condemned to a life of helpless idleness and misery. When he was ten a small school for the blind was opened at Nashville, a village six miles from the Campbells' home. His father went over to make inquiries about it ; but he came back sick at heart.

" I cannot do it," he said to the boy's mother, after telling her the cost of sending their blind boy to school.

" We must do it," said the brave-hearted mother ;

"it is the one thing we have been praying for ; we shall lose our chance ; the school will soon be full."

Setting to work with a will, she begged the help of neighbours ; a sewing meeting was held to make the boy's clothes ; and in twenty-four hours he was ready to start.

When Francis Campbell reached the school only one other pupil had arrived. When he was taken to the schoolroom a New Testament in raised letters was put into his hands, and he was so eager to learn that in less than an hour he had mastered the whole alphabet. Other pupils came afterwards, but none proved so apt as Campbell. One day the first singing lesson was given, and Campbell, as the brightest scholar, was called upon first. For some reason he was a hopeless failure, and after many attempts his teacher gave him up, declaring he could not tell one tune from another. After that, when the other boys were learning to sing and play the piano, young Campbell was set to basket and brush-making, and was teased about it unmercifully by his schoolfellows. In spite of the teacher's verdict, he vowed that he would master music, and secretly paid one of the other boys to teach him all the others were learning. Three months later the music-master, who was also blind, came into the room where young Campbell was practising on the piano.

"Who is that playing the new lesson so well ? " asked the master, and he received the surprise of his life when he discovered that this most promising pupil was the unmusical Campbell. Fifteen months afterwards Campbell won the school prize for piano playing.

Excelling his Sighted Brothers.

When home for the holidays the blind boy amazed his brothers, for he could beat them at almost anything, in spite of his blindness. He could hunt, fish, and climb as easily as they could, and was more daring and venturesome than any of them. The truth was that Francis Campbell had by this time resolved to prove that blindness need be no real handicap in life. With the bitter memories of his seven years of idleness and helplessness ever before him, it became the fixed plan of his life to teach the blind to lead normal lives of usefulness and freedom.

As a first step he vowed that he would secure a university education—an unheard-of thing for a blind youth. As his father had no means, the blind lad resolved to earn the money to secure this education, so he began giving music lessons. He secured two young ladies as pupils, but when they came for their first lesson he found himself helpless. In his enthusiasm he had overlooked one point—how was music written ? He knew how to teach a blind person, but how could he explain music and teach a sighted person ? He was absolutely at a loss, but was none the less determined to find the way. After a talk about music he dismissed his pupils, promising that they should make a proper beginning the following week. The week was spent in a desperate attempt to discover someone who would teach him how to teach sighted people. The day before his pupils were coming for their lesson, he had his first lesson in teaching music. From that day he never looked back. He became a successful music-teacher, all the while studying hard, bent on entering Harvard University.

Campbell's career at Harvard was a brilliant one, and he proved once for all that blindness need be no barrier to a good education. On leaving the University he secured an appointment as teacher in his own state, Tennessee. After two years' successful work, however, he was forced to leave the place, for a reason worth recording. From his earliest days Francis Campbell had been a strong opponent of slavery. One of his last recollections of sighted days was seeing his old coloured nurse, Aunt Maria, a slave, begging for mercy as she was horsewhipped for some minor offence.

"That vivid recollection just before I became quite blind influenced my whole life," he said afterwards, "and I have been an abolitionist ever since, thank God."

In Tennessee, when Campbell became a teacher, abolition was a burning question, and Campbell did not disguise the fact that as a Christian he was opposed to it. It was then discovered that he was actually teaching a negro to read—a terrible crime in the eyes of his enemies. First they tried to persuade him to change his views. When this failed, and he refused to give up teaching the negroes, they delivered an ultimatum :

"We give you twenty-four hours in which to reconsider your decision. If, at the end of that time, you still refuse, we shall string you up to the limb of the most convenient tree."

This threat failed to move him, and only his blindness saved him from lynch law. But although public opinion in Tennessee was against hanging a blind man, it had no objection to taking away his living. He found himself boycotted ; his pupils were all taken away by their parents, and he could get no new ones.

For the next ten years Campbell fought a hard fight in various States, trying to support himself and an invalid wife on his earnings, battling all the while against delicate health himself. Wherever he worked, he proved a pioneer in training the blind not merely to occupy themselves by employment, but to equip themselves to take leading positions in business and professional life.

A Tea-Meeting that Altered a Career.

When he was thirty-four his health broke down completely, and he was urged to take a trip to Europe. The Harvard Musical Association of Boston gave a grand concert in his aid, and he sailed with his wife and son for Liverpool, not merely to regain his health, but to study everything that concerned the blind. After eighteen months travelling in England and Germany he had not only regained his health but acquired a great deal of useful knowledge of books and appliances for teaching the blind. He booked his passage back to America at the beginning of 1871, and his last night in London was to be spent at a blind tea-meeting. This proved an ordinary charity affair, when "the poor blind" were regaled with tea and cakes. Campbell afterwards described it as the saddest evening he had ever spent. Talking with these blind people, he found that they were miserable and discontented with their aimless, empty lives. He went back to his hotel for the night, which was to be his last in England, haunted by the hopelessness of that blind crowd.

That tea-meeting was to alter the whole future life of Francis Campbell. Next morning he told his wife that they would not sail to America as planned. After breakfast he called on Dr. Armitage, a doctor who was nearly blind, and was using his wealth to found the British and Foreign Blind Association. That morning's conversation proved the beginning of a lifelong partnership in service on behalf of the blind. One day, as they were walking across Hyde Park, Campbell talked of his pioneer work in America, and outlined plans he was forming for further experiments.

"What will it cost to start a small school here and try these experiments for a couple of years," asked Dr. Armitage.

"Three thousand pounds," replied Campbell.

"I will give £1,000 if the other two can be raised," answered the doctor at once.

Campbell jumped at the chance, and the two men set to work, but it was found impossible to raise the other £2,000. Regretfully Campbell had to give up the idea of work in England, and began to pack up his belongings and prepare to depart. In the nick of time, however, some big gifts came in for the scheme, a fresh impetus was given to it, and within a few months the whole £3,000 was received.

Early in 1872, three small houses were taken near the Crystal Palace at Sydenham, for use as a school for the blind. Francis Campbell was appointed principal, with a free hand to apply his pioneer methods. From the beginning the school was a success, and eighteen months afterwards large new premises were secured and the present Royal Normal College for the Blind in Upper Norwood was established. Backed by Dr. Armitage, Campbell launched out with his new methods of work.

A New Method for the Blind.

With the unerring instinct of the pioneer, Francis Campbell had discovered the weak point in all previous attempts to educate the blind. Through lack of sports and physical pastimes, blind people were severely handicapped by a low condition of health. His own strenuous life in America had taught him the necessity for building up a strong physical body for his blind pupils. Only by this means, he believed, could they secure the courage, enterprise and ambition needed for winning success in business or professional life. So one of the novel features of the Royal Normal College was its gymnasium and swimming bath, and extensive grounds for outdoor recreation. Visitors to the College were amazed to find that the Principal gave as much time and thought to outdoor exercise for his students as for the musical and general educational work.

Five years after the College was opened its students were able to give musical performances in public, fully up to the standard of ordinary professional people possessing their sight. Within ten years of its founding, the pioneer methods introduced by Campbell won full recognition for the College in the educational world. Honours came to him, and in 1909 King Edward VII. knighted Dr. Campbell in recognition of the fact that the pioneer methods introduced by him had become part of the national system of education. To-day, although Sir Francis Campbell has passed on to his reward, the Royal Normal College for the Blind that he founded is carrying on his work, and is a city of light to those who live in darkness.

NOTES ON THE YARN.

Aim.

To show, through the work of Braille and Campbell, how new life and usefulness have been secured for blind people.

Historical.

Next to opening the eyes of the blind, there can be no greater blessing for those so afflicted than to be taught how to lead a normal, useful and happy life. The fact that this is now possible for sightless people is due to the high endeavours and indefatigable labour of men like Louis Braille and Sir Francis Campbell, LL.D. Both these pioneers owed the inception of their lifework to a desire to fulfil the Christian ideal of service. Though blind, they dedicated their lives to the service of their afflicted brothers and sisters, and it is largely due to their perseverance that to-day almost any walk in life is open to the blind. This means that instead of useless and idle dependence on the charity of others, the sightless can learn to become useful servants of the community.

Biographical.

Louis Braille was born January 4th, 1809, at Coupvray, Seine-et-Marne, twenty-three miles from Paris. At ten he was sent to the School for the Blind in Paris, and made good progress with his literary, musical and mathematical studies, learning to read by the embossed Roman type exclusively used at this period. Later he became an accomplished organist. In 1826 he was elected professor of the Blind Institution, and began by teaching grammar, geography and arithmetic, adding history, geometry, algebra and music later. After examining a new point system introduced by M. Barbier, he devoted all his time to improving this, and in 1829 published his first treatise explaining his system. Two years after his death, in 1852, the Braille system was officially adopted at the Paris School for the Blind. To-day there is hardly any system in use in blind schools which is not based on Braille, and although other means of blind writing and reading have been devised since, competent authorities consider that Louis Braille's system is still the best for all-round practical use.

Another inventor of a system of embossed reading for the blind was William Moon, born near Tunbridge Wells in 1818. Moon became blind through scarlet fever at twenty-one, and in 1839 perfected the "Moon system" of embossed reading. His work was thus almost contemporary with Louis Braille. The "Moon system" is a very simplified form of Roman type letters. In 1847 Moon started a monthly magazine for the blind and later opened the Moon Institution for the blind, deaf and dumb in Brighton. This work is still being carried on under the management of the National Institution for the Blind.

Francis Joseph Campbell, the father of modern education for the blind, was born in Franklin County, Tennessee, on October 9th, 1834. When a school for the blind was opened at Nashville in 1844, Campbell was one of its earliest pupils, but it was so badly organised and so poorly equipped, that in winter there was only one fire in the whole school, and young Campbell kept himself warm by strenuous physical exercise. This, and the hardy outdoor life in his mountain home, made the blind boy realise the great need for physical training for the sightless. He possessed boundless ambition, and probably out of his determination to secure a university education, and win a successful career for himself, came his unique contribution to the education of the blind. When he became a teacher in the Nashville School, the institution ran short of pupils, because parents did not see the necessity for educating blind children. This fact sent Campbell touring through the State of Tennessee on propaganda work, which must have been valuable training for his after-career. When Campbell's health broke down in 1868 he came to Europe, and made the acquaintance of Dr. Armitage, the well-known blind philanthropist, and the Royal Normal College for the Blind was founded in 1872.

Since the Great War the education of the blind has caught public attention by reason of the work undertaken by Sir Arthur Pearson and others on behalf of blinded soldiers, at institutes such as St. Dunstan's Hostel for the Blind, Regent's Park, London, N.W.

Questions.

What made Louis Braille devote his life to devising a system of blind-writing and reading?

How did Francis Campbell prove a pioneer teacher for the blind?

What is the greatest help that can be given to a blind person?

Which is the better method—to subscribe money to support the blind, or help to teach them how to be blind usefully?

V

WILLIAM WILBERFORCE

Dates : B., 1759 *: D.,* 1833.

" To Set at Liberty "

It was a bleak and blowy wintry day, but neither the gale nor the hail could scatter the great outdoor meeting in the Castle Yard at York. The beginning of 1784 was a stirring time in English politics, and regardless of the weather, thousands of the electors of Yorkshire had listened patiently throughout the short winter's day to speeches from Whigs, Tories and Coalitionists. On the high table that served as a platform, there suddenly climbed a boyish figure, so frail-looking that it seemed that he could scarcely stand against the violence of the gale, let alone hold his own in argument or win the attention of the great gathering.

" Who is he ? " Everyone seemed to be asking the question at once.

" The member for Hull—Wilberforce—returned at the last General Election."

Directly this new speaker began to address the assembly it was hushed to silence by the very charm of his voice, so perfectly pitched that every word reached the farthest fringe of the crowd, and so rich and varied in tone that men listened for the sheer joy of it. For over an hour he spoke with growing power, while the crowd listened spellbound. " He speaks like an angel," muttered one man admiringly.

Then came an interruption. A note was handed to the speaker, and scarcely pausing in his argument, the member for Hull mastered its contents at a glance. A minute later, waving the paper excitedly in the air, he cried :

" A message from the Prime Minister ! Parliament is dissolved ! Pitt has appealed to the people."

The meeting ended in a clamour of applause and excitement. Wilberforce that day had won the hearts of the Yorkshire freeholders. The famous critic Boswell was among that crowd, and said afterwards :

" I saw what seemed to me a shrimp mount upon the table ; but as I listened, he grew and grew until the shrimp became a whale."

As the yeomen of York scattered that day, they declared, " We will have this little man for our county member." And they did, for among the strangest of strange results of that election was the fact that William Wilberforce, an unknown young man, snatched a famous seat from the hands of the great county families, who had long regarded it as their own.

The Great Decision.

That scene in the Castle Yard at York proved a turning-point in Wilberforce's career in Parliament. The former member for Hull now represented the county of York, and became the bosom friend of Pitt, the " schoolboy Prime Minister." London society opened its arms to the attractive little member for York, and found him ready to talk and laugh, to sing a good song, to dance, to gamble, and to mimic well-known people with great skill and drollery. For a time it looked as though this young " blood " from the north, with plenty of gifts and plenty of money, would become a social butterfly and a popular politician, without a serious purpose in life.

The gaming-table had cast its spell over him, and his friends told him he was rich enough to play as often as he cared, win or lose. One night he " kept the bank " and when play was over discovered he had won £600. The amount meant little to him, but as he collected his winnings the anxiety and bitterness on the faces of the young men about him pulled him up sharply. In a flash he understood the situation—this money had been won from poor young men, and its loss was very serious to them ! He was touched to the quick as he realised that gambling is a sin against brotherhood, and he vowed there and then that he would give it up.

Soon afterwards Wilberforce went on a holiday jaunt that was to become the most serious journey of his life. He chose Isaac Milner as his companion, a Cambridge don who years before had been the usher of the grammar school he had attended at Hull.

Together they read the New Testament in Greek, with the result that new ideas began to work in Wilberforce's mind and the old joys of his former life failed to attract him. When he returned to London, the old ways of life became well-nigh unbearable.

" I must awake to my dangerous state, and never be at rest until I have made my peace with God," he wrote in his diary.

Soon after this he dedicated his life to the service of God. Henceforth he regarded his wealth as a trust to be used in the service of man, and his position in Parliament as a rare opportunity for the service of God. No more card-parties, no more Sunday suppers, no more theatres, no more of anything in his social life that was evil or tainted.

Then a strange thing happened—he still remained popular in Society, and was still sought after by hostesses, and still retained many of the friendships of his old life, including that of Pitt, the Prime Minister. The

truth was that his former friends discovered that, though
an avowed Christian, Wilberforce could still be jolly
and attractive, could still sing his ballads, and still be
the centre of all the fun, so long as it was clean and
kindly.

Of course some of his former friends had no use for
him and chaffed him about his conversion ; some of them
lectured him for always saying grace at meals, and for
humming hymn-tunes ; some called him a fool when they
discovered that he was pouring out his wealth to help
the unemployed, the destitute, and the orphan. But
none of them ever called him a prig, or a hypocrite—
some said he was a real Christian, and a saint.

Called to a Crusade.

One summer day, under an oak tree in the Prime
Minister's garden at Holwood, Wilberforce sat talking
with Pitt and his friend George Grenville. Below them
was the glorious Vale of Keston, but for once Wilberforce
had no eye for the beauty of the scene. He had long
waited for this interview with the Prime Minister, and
he was now looking for a chance of talking about a
subject dear to his heart. Suddenly Pitt turned to him
and exclaimed :

" Wilberforce, why don't you give notice of a motion
on the slave-trade ? You have taken such great pains
to collect evidence. Is not the subject admirably suited
to your character and talents ? "

Wilberforce was almost overcome with surprise and
delight. Clearly he was being divinely led to his great
crusade. That interview under the oak at Holwood was a
long one, for Pitt's abrupt question settled once for all
the career of Wilberforce, and he knew it.

" The first years that I was in Parliament I did nothing,"
he confessed to the two statesmen. " My own distinc-
tion was my darling object. Now I am determined to

do something big, something I can exercise my talents upon, something big enough to satisfy my conscience."

Wilberforce went on to tell them that he had always been stirred by the odious traffic in human lives, carried on under the name of the slave-trade. After his conversion a book written by Thomas Clarkson against the trade had fallen into his hands, and he had sent for the author to assure himself that the facts were true.

"The cause of the slaves at once made a strong appeal to me," declared Wilberforce, ready now to bare his heart to Pitt and Grenville, under the oak tree. "Here, if you like, is a big cause on which depends the welfare of hundreds of thousands of human beings. Here is a challenge which no Christian can evade. God Almighty has set before me two great objects, the suppression of the slave-trade and the reformation of manners."

As the three friends talked over the prospects of the fight in the House of Commons, none knew better than they that it would be a bitter and prolonged struggle—that one man alone must bear the burden of it, for no Government or party would dare to take it up. The struggle would mean the giving up of time and strength, the breaking of friendships, the facing of opposition and peril, the danger of arousing a storm that might destroy its author. Wilberforce knew all this, he had counted the cost, but nothing could hold him back.

Within a few days Clarkson and others, overjoyed at the news that Wilberforce had made the great decision, proclaimed from the house-tops their news :

"The Prime Minister's intimate friend has taken the field against the slave-trade."

At once the West Indian merchants and ship-owners, and others interested in this traffic in human liberty, took alarm and prepared to fight to the bitter end for what they called "the welfare of the West Indies, and

the prosperity of Britain's carrying trade on the high
seas."

During the whole of the following winter Wilberforce
worked hard preparing for his first attack on the slave-
trade. His first duty was to secure all possible evidence
of the cruelty of the traffic, and in this task he received
powerful aid from Thomas Clarkson, who went round
the ports collecting gruesome stories at first hand of
the cruelty of the slave-captains to their crew.

One day Clarkson called on Wilberforce, staggering
under a load of heavy iron leg-shackles, handcuffs,
thumbscrews and mouth-openers. Wilberforce gazed
with horror as these instruments of torture were spread
on the floor in front of him, and his face flushed with
anger as Clarkson told his story :

" I bought these from a shop in Liverpool that is well
patronised by the captains of slave ships. This valuable
evidence nearly cost me my life, for one night when I
was at the pier-head in Liverpool, a gang of eight or nine
slave-traders tried to throw me into the sea. I only
escaped death by the free use of my fists."

The Battle Royal.

On the eve of the great debate in Parliament, however,
when both sides were ready for battle, the champion of
the slaves was laid low. The frail little body of
Wilberforce had been broken in preparing for the battle.

" There's Wilberforce," said one man to another,
pointing to a little man who tottered towards his home
by the aid of a stout stick : " he can't last three weeks."

" He has no stamina to last a fortnight," declared an
eminent doctor to Wilberforce's mother, and he advised
the prompt removal of the dying man to Bath, on the
desperate chance that its healing waters might work a
miracle.

Wilberforce received the death sentence without

flinching. He was ready to go and die at Bath, if this was God's will, but one thing must be done before he left London, even if it killed him outright. Fighting against his weakness, he went to the Prime Minister and begged Pitt to take his place as champion of the slaves. Without hesitation, Pitt promised to do all that Wilberforce would have done. Deeply moved by the warm friendship and splendid loyalty of Pitt, the sick man left London and reached Bath in a state of collapse.

Then the miracle happened—Wilberforce began to mend and, once the corner was turned, to get well with remarkable rapidity. A month later he was able to begin the long carriage journey back to London. His full recovery was hastened by the glad news that a Bill had been passed into law, in the teeth of fierce opposition, limiting the number of slaves that could be carried on the slave ships, thus lessening the cruelty of overcrowding that was one of the worst features of the traffic.

When Wilberforce returned to Parliament some months later he was under no illusion as to the severity of the fight in front of him. The success of the Abolitionists in getting Parliament to limit the number of slaves carried on the ships had thoroughly alarmed the enemy. Like all men of evil, they loved darkness, and had done their utmost to prevent the facts of slavery being brought into the limelight of Parliament. Foiled in this, they now left no stone unturned to prove that slavery was a blessing for the negro and vital to the empire. In the press and at public meetings, they assured the British people that Abolition meant not only the end of our colonial empire, but the commercial downfall of the mother country.

When the great day came for Wilberforce to introduce his motion for the Abolition of the slave-traffic, the House of Commons was crowded. All eyes were fixed on the small, bent figure as Wilberforce arose in his seat to address the House. For three and a half hours they listened spellbound to the eloquent and beautiful voice of the champion of the slaves. In a speech that the orator Burke declared had not been equalled in modern times, Wilberforce exposed the horrible cruelty of the trade as violating the dictates of conscience, the principles of justice, and the laws of God.

The few great men in the House were all on Wilberforce's side, but the friends of the trade succeeded in getting the subject postponed, on the excuse that the House should hear evidence from witnesses before making a decision.

Thus began the long-drawn battle that was destined to last for many years, and to try the strength, patience and perseverance of Wilberforce to the utmost. Yet never once did he falter in his determination to smash the slave-trade. Nearly every year after that he brought in his Abolition Bill, and every time success was thwarted either by the indifference of his friends or the opposition of his enemies.

The Hazard of Duty.

Wilberforce was handicapped in his struggle for Abolition by the fact that he held a high ideal of Christian conduct. He firmly believed that a follower of Jesus Christ had no option but to live up to the teaching of Christ. We are not surprised, therefore, to find that he always " played the game," and was scrupulously fair in his methods even against the slave-traders. Early in the conflict, however, he discovered that many of them would stick at nothing. Most of the men engaged in the trade had perforce been brutalised by it and on more than one occasion his life was threatened, but bullies are proverbial cowards, and the absolute fearlessness of the slaves' champion saved his life.

One day the captain of a slave ship thought to destroy their enemy by legal murder, so challenged Wilberforce to a duel. The plot was a clever one, for duelling was then common, and on such a point of honour public men of the time were very sensitive. The captain, however, had forgotten the conscience of Wilberforce, and was staggered by his refusal to fight. He was still further amazed to find that taunts of " coward " failed to bring his opponent up to duelling-point. The Christian principles of Wilberforce, which he had never attempted to hide, enabled him to refuse to fight a duel and yet retain his honour and reputation.

On another occasion a slave-captain who had been denounced for barbarous cruelty by Wilberfore, became very threatening. This rascal lay in wait for Wilberforce and demanded, quite civilly at first, " a public apology, £5,000 in cash, and a place under Government." Finding that his victim would neither give nor promise him anything, he became abusive, and followed the M.P. to his home, uttering dire threats. Wilberforce was quite unmoved, even when the man called several times at his house and was so threatening that the servants trembled for their master's safety. Wilberforce knew he was comparatively safe in London, since he was so much in the public eye. Presently, however, he had occasion to travel to York, which would be very dangerous, but he was quite unmoved by his friends' fears.

"I can't say I fear much," he said bravely, " and if he were to commit any act of violence, it would be helpful rather than injure the cause."

That was just like Wilberforce, strong in the over-shadowing presence of God—he was not thinking of himself—his thoughts first, last and all the time were of the cause of the freedom of the slaves.

In spite of his protests his friends would not hear of his travelling alone unarmed, and Lord Rokeby insisted on acting as his armed escort, so when Wilberforce started in his carriage for York, Rokeby travelled with him, with the business end of a large pistol sticking out of his pocket for everyone to see.

Attempts were also made by his enemies to drag his name in the mire of evil slander and assaults on his character. He was said to be a cruel husband and a wife-beater ; others said his wife was a negress. Wilberforce laughed heartily at these scandals, for he was a bachelor. But when the story was spread that he had thrown up the cause through faint-heartedness, he leapt at once to the challenge and denounced the lie :

" A man who fears God is not at liberty to give up," he declared, thus revealing the secret of his brave perseverance.

Victory at Last.

Year after year passed, but in spite of distractions at home and war abroad, neither Government nor people were allowed to forget that the sin against human brotherhood—slavery—was still going on. In season and out of season, Wilberforce and his friends kept the subject alive, and his constant speeches in Parliament were doing far more than he knew to work a silent change in public opinion.

Nine years after his first attempt, Wilberforce arose in the House of Commons to move once more his bill against the slave traffic. When he had finished speaking he had a great reception, for everyone knew he was at last going to win. Enthusiasm rose steadily until at the close of the debate the Solicitor-General, turning to Wilberforce, declared :

" This night you will lay your head on the pillow a happy man, with the knowledge that innumerable voices will be raised in every quarter of the world to bless you."

The end of this speech was lost as the whole House jumped to its feet, giving Wilberforce round after round of cheers until the roof re-echoed.

It was the supreme moment of Wilberforce's life. Years of struggle had at last given him the victory. Overcome with emotion, the little man with the great heart sat bent in his seat, his head in his hands, with the tears streaming down his face as he thanked God for the victory. In his home that night his comrades in the great fight gathered to celebrate the victory.

" Let us make out the names of those sixteen miscreants who voted against the Bill," cried someone.

" Never mind the miserable sixteen," cried Wilberforce ; " let us think of the glorious 283 who voted for us."

When his friends had departed, Wilberforce fell upon his knees and poured out his soul in humility and gratitude for that day's great triumph of the cause. Even in this moment of the greatest victory of his life his great heart was free from vanity or self-glory. The entry in his private diary records only his thanksgiving to the " Giver of all good " and gratitude to the British people—" God will bless this country," he wrote.

" God bless Massa Wilb'foss," was the fervent prayer of numberless negroes when the news spread like wildfire through the West Indian plantations of the great victory of their champion.

* * * * *

Nearly thirty years later, as Wilberforce lay on his death-bed, he received the glad news that a Bill for the abolition of slavery itself under the British Flag had been passed by the House of Commons. It was a fitting moment for the passing of his great soul, and he thanked God that he had been permitted to see that day of triumph—" Lord, now lettest Thou Thy servant depart in peace."

NOTES ON THE YARN.

Aim.

To show how Wilberforce, in applying the teaching of Jesus on the brotherhood of man, fought against the slave-trade until he won a great victory for human liberty.

Biographical.

A passionate devotion to the teaching of Jesus that "all men are brethren" is the outstanding feature of the life and work of William Wilberforce. Back of all his long and tedious fight for the abolition of slavery and other social sins against brotherhood, was the conviction that neither the nation nor the individual could be Christian in the real sense unless the Golden Rule governed all relationships of man to man. It will be seen that the life of Wilberforce can be made a thrilling story of the pioneer who, daring all peril, defying all opposition, and grappling with all difficulty, blazes out a path for God and righteousness through the jungle of ignorance, greed and oppression. We must aim to show that the more spectacular and well-known champions of liberty and conquerors of the slave-trade were but following the trail of Wilberforce. Pressing along the road he made, are not only the great Missionary Societies of to-day, but educational and social workers who take human brotherhood for granted, whereas Wilberforce was scoffed at for suggesting such a Utopian doctrine.

William Wilberforce was born at Hull on August 24th, 1759; son of a wealthy merchant, he was left fatherless at nine, and his mother's only thought was to educate him for fashionable society. Delicate in health, he was quick-witted and high-spirited, and on entering St. John's College, Cambridge, at seventeen, made a very unfortunate start : " On the very first night of my arrival I was introduced to as licentious a set of men as can well be conceived," he bitterly complained afterwards. After wasting nearly twelve months with this set he pulled himself together, and in due time passed his exams. with credit. He had made the acquaintance of William Pitt (the younger) at Cambridge, and they became friends for life. In 1780 Wilberforce entered Parliament as Member for Hull; throughout his parliamentary career, which lasted forty-five years, he remained an Independent, and was never a party man, although his friendship for Pitt made him in a real sense " the first and greatest of the Pittites." In 1784 he was returned to Parliament for both Hull and Yorkshire, but chose to represent the county. In the following year he made a tour of the Continent with a party that included Isaac Milner, Dean of Carlisle, and under the Dean's influence, after a long process of spiritual turmoil, he became " soundly converted " at the age of twenty-six. Intensely sincere and practical, Wilberforce began simply and directly to practise the Christian life in the position where he felt God had placed him ; he did not turn away from the world in disgust ; he simply dedicated his wealth, social position and place in Parliament to the service of Christ and the welfare of mankind. His first practical step was to form a society for improving morals. Soon afterwards a self-constituted Committee for the Abolition of the Slave-Trade, which had developed from a group of Quakers, began an active propaganda to arouse the press, the public, and Parliament, and before long, through a variety of ways that clearly constituted a Divine call, Wilberforce dedicated his private life and public career to the abolition of the traffic in slaves, as a first step towards the banishing of slavery altogether. Throughout the long struggle Wilberforce was backed up by the Abolition Committee in general and Thomas Clarkson in particular; he sacrificed everything, health included, in preparing evidence strong and definite enough to carry an Abolition Bill through Parliament against the tremendous opposition of vested interests, the lethargy of the average Member and of the general public, and the preoccupation and dilatoriness of the Parliamentary machine. Wilberforce's speech introducing his first Abolition Bill was made on May 12th, 1798, and it was not until March 25th, 1807, that the Bill at last became law. Wilberforce was forty-eight at this time, and though he lived to seventy-four, the rest of his life was by no means an anti-climax, for he laboured as indefatigably as ever to secure the abolition of the trade abroad and the stopping of the institution of slavery entirely.

Slavery.

Slavery is probably as old an evil as war, since it must have begun in primitive times with the discovery that it was more profitable to keep captives in servitude than massacre them. Slavery was permitted by the Old Testament Law, and although it is never denounced in the New Testament, the teaching of Jesus on human relationships clearly contains the germ that at long last developed in the Christian conscience into the recognition that it is a sin against both the Fatherhood of God and the brotherhood of man. The modern practice of negro slavery began early in the sixteenth century, through the fact that the aborigines of America proved too weak for the labour required by Portuguese settlers in the recently discovered New World. Sir John Hawkins was the first English-man to engage in the traffic, which soon assumed large proportions under the British Flag, England exporting no fewer than 300,000 slaves from Africa between 1680 and 1700. The slave ships were so overcrowded that often the slaves had not room to lie flat on their backs, but were packed together on broad shelves between decks, in sultry heat and rank air, so that sometimes a quarter of them died on the voyage. Those who survived became the chattels of their owners, with no more rights than cattle, and although legal restraints were imposed to protect the slaves, these had little ameliorative value. From the early fathers onwards, the Church had always condoned slavery, so that when the system was first denounced (chiefly by Quakers) little headway was made in either Britain or America, until in 1787 the Abolition Committee began its task of informing public opinion as to the facts.

Book of Reference.

Wilberforce—A Narrative, by R. Coupland (Oxford Press, 1923).

Questions for Discussion.

What led to the great change in Wilberforce's life ?
Why was he asked to champion the slaves ?
What made his fight so trying and so dangerous ?
On what grounds did Wilberforce base his case for Abolition ?
Are there any forms of human labour to-day that are akin to slavery ?

VI

SIR RICHARD TANGYE

Dates : B., 1833 *: D.,* 1906.

A " DOER OF THE WORD "

As the " Puffing Billy " clanked and squeaked its way to the Tin Mine, it belched forth volumes of white steam and black smoke, and sent sparks of fire high into the air. This bit of railway line in Cornwall was one of the first to be opened, and although the primitive engine could do its thirty miles an hour, it did it so clumsily that it was an object of terror and superstitious dread to most people. No wonder, then, that little Richard Tangye and his brothers kept very close to their nurse as " Billy " puffed his way across the corner of their father's farm.

" It is a wicked thing," said Jennefer, the nurse-girl, to the Tangye boys, " and you must learn to hate it, because it makes more smoke and fire to torment the poor sinners in hell."

Richard was a queer little chap, who said little but thought a great deal. Jennefer's remark set him thinking so hard that he never forgot her words, and after that he watched with awe when " Puffing Billy " passed.

From both his father and grandfather, Richard Tangye and his brothers inherited an interest in engines and machinery. Richard loved to hear his father tell of that exciting night when he saw William Murdock try his first railway-engine in the little lane in front of the Tangye's cottage at Redruth.

" Murdock had built the little locomotive in his own cottage," Joseph Tangye would tell his boys. " One night after his work was done at the mines, Murdock went out with his model to the lane leading to the church, to try it. Having lit the lamp, the water soon boiled, and off started the engine. Murdock ran after it, but it outran him. It went past our cottage at a great rate, with the inventor running after it. Presently we heard distant shouts of terror, and found afterwards that the vicar had been scared by the engine, thinking that the hissing, spitting little demon was no other than the evil one himself."

Richard shared the pride of his family that the first locomotive that ever ran in England made its trial trip in front of their cottage.

His father had worked in a mine before he became a farmer, and often talked to the boys about his work underground, but in Richard's eyes his grandfather was much more wonderful, for in spite of his age he still worked as a night driver of a mine pumping engine. His grandfather was a tall, active old man, who used to say to the boys :

" Hard work never killed anybody. I drove the engine for ten hours, worked on the farm seven hours, and wasted the rest."

" Pick Your Heels Up."

On Sundays the whole family were marched to the Methodist chapel in their best clothes, the tall old grandfather bringing up the rear, and cutting quite a smart figure in a blue tail-coat, with bright brass buttons and a high collar. As they went along it sometimes happened that Richard walked carelessly.

" Pick your heels up ! " the old man would call out.

So often did young Richard have to be pulled up for careless walking, that these words were branded on his memory. It often happened in later life, when things were not going well, or Richard Tangye was tempted to be slack in his work, he seemed to hear his grandfather's sharp reproof : " Pick your heels up ! " and was spurred on to fresh exertions.

About this time Richard met with an accident one day that probably altered his whole life. Whilst playing at school he slipped down and broke his right arm. There was a great hue and cry—his mother was sent for, and in alarm she hurried the boy, half-faint with pain and shock, to the village doctor.

" He will never be able to earn his living by hard work with his hands," said the doctor as he set the broken limb ; then, seeing the mother's alarm, he added consolingly : " He has a good-sized head ; try what a little extra schooling will do for him ! "

So it came about that Richard's accident proved a blessing in disguise. Instead of being taken from school at an early age to earn his living at a blacksmith's or in a wheelwright's workshop, like his elder brothers, Richard was sent to a better school for two or three years. Here he felt he must do his best to justify the hopes and expectations of his parents, by showing that he had brains in " the good-sized head " that had won the approval of the doctor. By hard work he soon made good progress, and began to take an interest in the great world outside. One day he spent a halfpenny on his first newspaper, a small sheet published in Bristol. He devoured its news with keen interest, and tucked away in one corner he found a little piece of advice that stuck to him ever afterwards—it was this :

" Everyone can do something for the public, if it is only to pick a piece of orange-peel off the pavement."

Big doors swing on little hinges, and that little paragraph set Richard Tangye thinking. It led him to the discovery that self-help, and getting on, were not the only things in life, and that no man is worth his salt if he does not do something to help other people.

Finding that Richard's extra schooling was justified by the progress he was making, his parents scraped together the money to send him to a Quaker boarding-school at Sidcot, near Bristol, when he was fourteen. At fifteen he became a pupil teacher, at a salary of five shillings per quarter. As the years passed he felt more and more that it was in engineering that his bent lay, and in 1851, while he was at home for his summer holiday, an event happened which settled this question.

"I am going up to London to see the Great Exhibition," exclaimed his brother James one day, rushing into the house in great excitement, and waving a five-pound note in his hand which his employer had given him ; "and what's more, I intend to take you with me, Richard."

A few days later, in the gathering twilight in London, two young men were seen peering through the glass wall of the glittering palace in Hyde Park, feasting their eyes on the big steam-engine that was one of the chief exhibits in the engineering section. They were Richard Tangye and his brother. They had only arrived in London that evening, and though tired with the long journey, they could not stop to eat or rest until they had had a first peep at the Exhibition. During the next few days they explored the Exhibition from end to end, and, as Richard put it, saw all the sights of London that could be seen without payment.

Those wonderful days in the great metropolis, with its marvels of engineering, made Richard more discontented then ever with his work at school. He left no stone unturned to secure his freedom, and at sixteen he persuaded his parents and the school authorities to release him from Sidcot. He arrived home rejoicing in his freedom, but his high spirits soon gave place to despair.

" I suddenly realised that I was face to face with the world," he said afterwards, " with but few friends who could help me, and with no business experience."

Like his brothers he had plenty of ambition, but, unlike them, his powerless right arm prevented him from hammering cheerfully at wheels and horseshoes until the way opened for something better. His desire to get on and make the best of his life had been fed by reading the lives of men like Benjamin Franklin, and by his close study of the Bible, with its stories of Joseph and David, and other heroes who climbed to high position by faith and hard work.

Alone in Birmingham.

One day his eye caught an advertisement of a vacancy for a clerk in a small engineering works in Birmingham, and although it was a long way from home he applied for the post—and got it. A few weeks later, this lad of sixteen set out to begin life alone in the city of Birmingham, full of terror at the prospect. It was winter, the streets were ankle-deep in mud, and the griminess of the busy city smote the country boy with dismay.

Next morning, when he set out to work, another bitter blow awaited him. In contrast to the large engineering works of his dreams, he found that the business he sought was conducted in a tiny house up a narrow lane, in the smokiest and most grimy part of the town. The office was in a loft, which was approached by a step-ladder, and he found his new employer standing at his desk in hat and overcoat to keep himself warm.

"I am glad you have turned up," he said, when Richard Tangye tremblingly explained his errand ; " will you copy these invoices ? "

In a big town a boy from the country finds plenty of temptation without looking for it. In those days there were no free libraries or institutes where evenings could

c

be profitably employed, but there were plenty of music-halls and public-houses, where temptation abounded. But Richard Tangye had learned to serve God, and knew where to look for help to overcome temptation, and had not been sent out to face life without good advice.

"Make straight paths to thyself," his mother had often told him; adding, "Richard, if you ever get money, never let money get you."

One of the leading men at the Friends' Meeting House where Richard had regularly worshipped with his parents, had given him this piece of parting advice:

"Richard, thou art going to a large town where there are many temptations. Thy father has left thee a good name, and it is an unusual one. It is not like Jones or Brown; and if thou doest anything wrong, everyone will know who it is. See that thou keep it bright. Begin to give as soon as thou begins to get."

Steering clear of places of temptation, Richard spent his evenings in studying all the newspapers and books he could get hold of, and soon began to turn the information gained to good account.

A year later the young clerk had done much to develop his master's business, and had also brought his elder brothers from Cornwall, James being foreman of the works, George clerk of the works, and Joseph had started a new department. The engineering skill of these three, added to Richard's business ability, soon increased the output so much that more money was needed, and their employer took a partner with plenty of capital. Up to this point Richard had been trusted by his employer, but the new partner put a new window in the office, so that he could keep a strict eye on Richard's work. Richard objected to being watched, and said he could not work for a man who did not trust him, so promptly resigned.

Instead of seeking a new master, he determined to

plunge into business for himself as a merchant, and with a bag of samples of bolts, nails, etc., found his way back to Cornwall in search of orders. People soon found that they could trust Richard Tangye, that he was honest in business, that his word could be relied upon, and that he was not ashamed to be called a Christian.

Soon after this, he induced his brothers to join him, thus changing the business from " Richard Tangye, General Merchant," to " Tangye Brothers, Engineers."

Launching "The Great Eastern."

One dark winter's night Richard was startled by a loud ring at the door-bell. Opening the door, a gentleman stood on the step, who, after peering into the little workshop, said : " I am sorry ; I've made a mistake " ; and turned to go.

" Whose place are you looking for, sir ? " asked Richard.

" Tangyes'," replied the man.

He was at once invited in, and explained that he had been sent by Brunel, the famous engineer, who wanted a special " jack " (lifting machine) that James Tangye had patented. Far into the night the brothers talked with the stranger, whose visit proved the start of an enormous leap forward for " Tangye Bros." Brunel had built a mammoth paddle-steamer, which he called the *Great Eastern*, but could not launch it. The ship beat all records for size, and was so large that it could not be launched in the ordinary way, so the great engineer had sent for the help of Tangye Brothers. After a long struggle against many difficulties, the *Great Eastern* finally took the water easily, but not before two dozen of Tangye's patent " jacks " had been specially made for the job.

" We launched the *Great Eastern* and the *Great Eastern* launched us," Richard used to say afterwards, and it was perfectly true. The fame of the engineering brothers spread far and wide as the story of the triumph of their "jacks" became known. From that time the business moved steadily forward. The brothers were constantly inventing or improving new machinery, while Richard was kept busy getting orders and running the business. Greatly daring, they engaged their first workman, but carefully explained that they could not promise him more than three months' work. Long before the three months were up they had to call in more workmen. Not only in Britain, but from Europe and America, orders came for engines and machinery, for people discovered that the work done by Tangyes was of the very best, for the name of Tangye on a machine was a guarantee of good work.

One day a gentleman called at Tangyes' with a design for a new lifting block he had invented.

"I have been to every mechanical engineer in the city, and none of them can make it work properly," he said, "and I have been advised to come to you as a last resort. I am told that if you can't do it, no one can."

The Tangye brothers took the job on, promising to do their best. Day after day the four brothers put their heads together and worked at the block, but every time they failed. The inventor was in despair, but the brothers would not give it up. After weeks of experimenting and experimenting again, the inventor lost heart and went off, but George Tangye would never admit defeat, and worked on the invention for several months. At last he believed he had discovered the cause of failure, and the inventor was hurriedly fetched. Richard had such faith in his brother's skill that he prepared a contract that would give them sole rights for making the pulley. The result was that at one o'clock in the morning, when Richard was working in the office, he heard a great shout from the workshop, and hurrying across the yard he found his brothers and the inventor standing in triumph round the pulley, which was working successfully at last.

Twenty years later, Richard Tangye was head of one of the biggest engineering firms in the world. Thousands of workmen were employed at the works, and he and his brothers were rich men. But Richard still remembered his mother's last words : " Make straight paths for thyself ; if you ever get money, never let money get you." Never for a moment did he forget that he and his brothers had risen from the ranks of the workers. Always he treated his workmen as comrades in industry, not as machines to add to his wealth. Believing that a Christian employer should apply the teachings of Jesus to his business, Richard became a pioneer in improving the lot of factory workers ! He built a large dining-hall, so that his workmen could eat their midday meal in comfort, and amid cleanly surroundings, instead of in the dirt and dust of the workshop. He started classes and provided teachers so that they could gain promotion by better education. He not only paid them good wages, but gave them part of the profits of the business.

The Nine-Hour Day.

The time came when the workers in many places came out on strike because their employers refused their demand for " a nine-hours' day." As soon as he heard of this, Richard Tangye took quick action. So far, the workmen of Birmingham had done nothing more than talk among themselves about the nine-hour day. One morning they were surprised to hear the dinner-hour signal fifteen minutes before it was due, and to be called together into the principal workshop. Here Richard Tangye addressed them on the nine-hour day question, and announced that he and his brothers had decided to give them at once the nine-hour day unasked. That night the workmen paraded the streets of Birmingham headed by a large banner on which was boldly printed the words : " Nine hours given without asking by Tangye Brothers." Other Birmingham employers at first refused to listen to the nine-hour demand, but the example of Richard Tangye proved more forcible than the strike threats of their workmen, and the victory for a nine-hour day was won in Birmingham without a strike.

Because he was so genuinely Christian, Richard Tangye never attempted to lower his standard for the sake of getting orders, or making more money, as the following story will show. Among his best customers was a man who used foul language ; an oath seemed to find a place in almost every sentence. At the risk of losing a good customer, Richard felt compelled to protest, so one day said pleasantly :

" You would very much oblige me if, before entering my office, you would kindly scrape the oaths off ; you will find a scraper at the door."

The customer looked him straight in the face and stammered : " Do you mean it ? "

" I do," said Richard boldly.

" I believe you," said the customer, " but there is so much cant about I was suspicious. I will do as you say."

Occasionally after that he would lapse into his old habit and use an oath, but would immediately apologise : " I beg your pardon ; I had forgotten the scraper."

The heavy work of running a huge engineering business was not allowed to take all Richard Tangye's time and attention. The advice of his old Quaker friend, " Begin to give as soon as thou begins to get," became a habit with him. Time would fail to tell of all his generous gifts. Loyalty to Jesus Christ produced within him a strong sense of public duty, and as he made his money in Birmingham he felt he ought to throw himself heart and soul into its religious and municipal life. He became a member of the local School Board and Town Council, and worked hard to secure for the people the fullest possible benefits from popular education. To the end of his days he was a generous benefactor to education and a benevolent friend to all good causes. He had repeatedly to refuse Parliamentary honours, and as long as he could, postponed the knighthood that he so richly deserved. When he died, Dr. Guinness Rogers, the distinguished Congregational minister, paid him this tribute :

" His religion was not a matter of creeds or churches, but of life. It entered into all his relations and activities. It would be hard to find a man more anxious to ' do justly, love mercy and walk humbly with God.' "

NOTES ON THE YARN.

Aim.

To show how Richard Tangye proved himself a genuine Christian, unspoiled by success in business, holding his riches and power as a trust for God.

Biographical.

The whole life of Sir Richard Tangye, it will be seen, is an illuminating example of the result of applying the teachings of Jesus to business and everyday life. At a time when so many professing Christians seem content to put away much of their Christianity with their Sunday clothes, the object lesson of the life of Richard Tangye is a powerful rebuke of the excuse that " the Sermon on the Mount is not practical." When the youth, Richard Tangye, dedicated his life to Jesus Christ, he applied his Master's teaching to the preparation of an engineering career ; and when perseverance and ingenuity brought success, he still faithfully applied the principles of Jesus Christ in carrying on a great business. In his hobbies and recreations he showed that a good Christian can be an all-round cultured man, while his philanthropy and practical goodness are an example of how a Christian should regard his worldly wealth as a trust.

Richard Tangye was born at Illogan, near Redruth, Cornwall, on November 24th, 1833, at a time when the echoes of the Reform Bill still lingered in the Duchy, and the uplifting appeal of the Methodist Revival was still being felt. He came of a long-lived, sturdy family, " poor and pious," to use a hackneyed phrase. Richard was one of five brothers, two of them older than himself, and all of them intensely interested in engineering. Breaking his arm when nine years old, Richard could never work with his hands as the others did, but in a broad sense was " the brains of the family." With fear and trembling he plunged into the engineering world of Birmingham at sixteen as junior clerk. Within three years

Richard again proved himself the pioneer of the family, possessing sturdy independence and initiative, for he started business for himself as a merchant. Within a year he had induced his brother Joseph to join him as an engineer. From this humble beginning grew the great firm of Tangyes, Ltd., of Cornwall Works, Birmingham. From its inception Richard proved the brains of the business, although he himself would have modestly ascribed its success to the ingenuity and skill of his engineering brothers. The fact is that the four brothers always worked together as a happy team, each living up to the motto Richard had chosen for himself when a lad : "Industry and uprightness." Neither Richard nor his brothers forgot "the pit whence they were digged," and from the start they treated their workmen with consideration. Richard in particular proved a pioneer in improving the conditions of industry, humanising the relations between employer and employed by providing social amenities, educational classes, shorter working hours, and a system of co-partnership or profit sharing.

Richard Tangye was throughout his life very closely associated with the Society of Friends. He came of Methodist stock, but his parents became Quakers, and under their influence a sterling religious character developed. His Christian discipleship led him to become a leader and benefactor in the public life of Birmingham. He died on October 14th, 1906, in retirement in his own county, Cornwall.

The beginning of the railway era about 1813 led to an enormous development in British trade and industry, and it was the good fortune of Richard Tangye and his brothers to start business at this critical time. The introduction of machinery, which had been steadily developing during the preceding twenty years, not only revolutionised the industrial life of the country, but afforded tremendous scope for clever and ingenious engineers. Steam was being harnessed to machine after machine, annihilating toil and bridging time and space in a way truly marvellous. The factory system came in with a bound, with the result that capitalists amassed fortunes by exploiting the labour of men, women, and little children, until the humane efforts of public-spirited men, and the agitation of the workers themselves, wrung from Parliament the Factory Acts and other industrial legislation. The relations of Capital and Labour have been regularised, and to some extent improved, by Act of Parliament, but our yarn shows how a Christian capitalist could anticipate legislation by pioneer work in this direction.

Questions.

What was the good advice given to Tangye when he started life ?
What were his " secrets of success " ?
How did he prove a pioneer in industrial life ?
What is the lesson of his life ?

VII

WILLIAM PENN

Dates : B., 1644 *: D.,* 1718.

"The Holy Experiment"

When Van Tromp fixed a broom to his mast-head and boasted that he would sweep the English from the seas, the Dutchman had not reckoned with the pugnacity and courage of the English admirals. Every schoolboy knows that it was Van Tromp who was swept off the seas by Blake, but it is not so well known that Admiral Penn had much to do with the English victory. Penn stood next in rank to Blake, and on the latter's death Oliver Cromwell, champion of English liberty, made Admiral Penn his general at sea. After the Restoration the admiral became Sir William Penn, through his victory over the Dutch.

Meanwhile, a small boy, also named William Penn, was growing up in the admiral's home on Tower Hill, and must have listened eagerly as his mother related stories of his father's gallantry at sea. She must have told him stories, too, of the courage and victories of Cromwell and his Ironsides in the battles waged on land for liberty of conscience and freedom. In this way courage was developed in young William Penn, and a passion for liberty that was to make him a successful leader in a great fight of quite another order later on.

The boy was sent to the Grammar School at Chigwell where the founder had stipulated that :

" The master should be a good poet, of a sound religion, neither papal nor Puritan ; no tippler, nor haunter of ale-houses, no puffer of tobacco, and above all apt to teach, and severe in his government."

Under such a master young Penn studied Greek and Latin until he was twelve, when he had a private tutor at home. Then came a strange experience. One night his room seemed suddenly flooded with light, and in some peculiar way he not only felt in God's presence, but called to a holy life. The vision faded, but it seemed to young Penn that the light remained with him, guiding him throughout his life. With the courage and pertinacity that he inherited from his father, he vowed that he would walk by this inner light and obey the voice of conscience whatever happened.

A year or two later he was sent to Oxford and made friends with a group of students who were attracted by the new teaching of George Fox, whose followers were beginning to be called Quakers. Before long Penn and his friends refused to go to church with the other students, for they desired to worship God in their own way. But as the law compelled all subjects of the King to conform to State worship, Penn and his friends were heavily fined for non-conformity.

Soon afterwards the King ordered that surplices should be worn in church. This proved too much for the simple tastes of Penn and his friends, and in a wild moment they swooped down on some students going to church in surplices, and tore the offending garments from their backs. For this disgraceful behaviour Penn and the other offenders were publicly expelled from college.

When Penn arrived home in disgrace, his father was very angry. Called upon to explain his conduct, the young man made his father still angrier by trying to defend his conduct on the ground that he intended to become a Quaker. This was more than the admiral could stand. He thrashed his son with a cane and, finding him still unrepentant, turned him out of doors. In vain did the mother plead for her boy, for to the admiral, as to so many people at that time, there could hardly be a greater crime or disgrace than to be related to a Quaker.

Soldier or Quaker ?

Determined to cure his son of this strange religion, the admiral sent him to Ireland to take charge of some family estates there. Young Penn soon showed that his religious convictions did not prevent him from being a good man of business, for the admiral learned that William was not only managing his father's affairs most successfully, but was acting for the Government. The next bit of news from Ireland made his father's heart glow with pride, for when an insurrection broke out William joined the army that was being raised to suppress it. The admiral's hopes rose still higher when he received a portrait of his wayward son, dressed in a suit of armour, " an exceedingly handsome officer with hair parted in the middle, profuse dark locks falling over his shoulders and a neckcloth of fine lace hanging down the front of his polished breastplate." Alas for the admiral's hopes ! The next report showed that his son had given up being a soldier in order to become a Quaker. Hearing that Thomas Loe, a Quaker who had deeply impressed him years before, was preaching in Cork, young William Penn had travelled post-haste to hear him, with the result that he joined the Society of Friends formed by George Fox.

Young Penn was soon to discover what it meant to be a Quaker. While attending a meeting of the Friends in Cork a soldier entered and tried to break up the meeting. With rising wrath Penn seized him by the collar, and was about to throw him down the stairs when the others stopped him.

"Friends are peaceable people, and do not do such things," they said to the abashed Penn, who had to learn that the new society he had joined refused to fight or use force. Therefore, when the soldier brought back some officers and other soldiers, the whole party were marched off to jail, and this time Penn made no resistance.

When released from prison, Penn returned home and told his father he had now become a Quaker. The admiral became very angry, and as soon as his son began using "thee" and "thou" (as all the Quakers did) he flew into a terrible rage.

"You may 'thee' and 'thou' whom you please except the King, the Duke of York, and myself—these thou shalt not 'thee' and 'thou.'"

Finding that storming and threats failed to move his son, the admiral disowned him, and turned him out of doors penniless. Starvation now stared young Penn in the face, for as the son of a rich man he had no skill or trade to earn a living. Not for one moment, however, would he think of giving in to his father, and he might have starved but for his mother, who secretly supplied him with food. He spent the next few months in travelling the country, preaching for the Quakers, and he wrote a book in support of their teaching. In time he became one of the leaders of this new sect, and soon had to suffer persecution with them, for he was charged with heresy by the Bishop of London and locked in the Tower. For eight long months he remained in a gloomy dungeon, and used the time to write his famous book, "No Cross, no Crown." One day his father sent a servant with a message that he thought would bring his son to his "senses."

"The Bishop of London has declared that you shall either recant, or die a prisoner," was the message.

William Penn was not to be frightened by anything that man could do, and without hesitation replied :

" Thou mayest tell my father that my prison shall be my grave before I will budge a jot, for I owe obedience to my conscience to no mortal man."

The Right of Free Worship.

The gallant old admiral knew a brave man when he met one, and finding his son would face death rather than give up his religion, he eventually received him again into his home.

Not long after this, William Penn received a shock of surprise. Going one day to the Meeting House in Gracechurch Street to worship after the manner of the Society of Friends, he found the door padlocked, and a number of soldiers on duty outside. This was a new move on the part of the authorities against the Quakers, and Penn at once took up the challenge against this invasion of religious liberty.

Unable to get inside to worship, he began to preach to the crowd that collected in the street outside, with the result that he and another Friend were promptly arrested and marched off to Newgate. The sequel to this arrest is recorded to-day on a stone tablet that adorns the wall of the new court of justice in the Old Bailey that stands on the site of Newgate Prison. The scene at Penn's trial has become famous. The magistrates soon found that Penn knew enough of English law to make it difficult for them to make out a case against him, and the twelve jurymen gave the verdict of " Guilty of speaking in Gracechurch Street." For two days the jury were kept locked up without meat, drink, fire or tobacco, because they refused to obey the judge, who ordered them to find Penn guilty of speaking to an unlawful assembly. The jurymen would not give way, however, and in the end were fined and imprisoned "for contempt of court." The case caused a great stir, for both Penn and the jury were in the right, and eventually all were set at liberty.

As the years passed Penn became the champion of the Quakers. Inheriting the name and fortune of a great English admiral, he could count the King as one of his friends, in spite of the fact that he had powerful enemies because he was ever ready to stand up for religious liberty. He now occupied too high a position to be persecuted or imprisoned, but he was ever ready to take up the case of poor and unknown Quakers who had to suffer for conscience' sake. In spite of his wealth and social standing he lived the life of a simple Christian, working harder than any labourer in writing and journeying all over the country, preaching and teaching.

At this time many Quakers were following the footsteps of the Pilgrim Fathers; persecuted and harassed in England, they fled to the New World to find liberty to worship God in their own way. This led William Penn to embark upon his "Holy Experiment," a piece of pioneer work that has made his name famous. He had inherited claims on the King for money lent by his father, so he conceived the bold plan of securing a grant of land in the New World from His Majesty, in payment of the debt. Penn's object was not to pile up more wealth, but to found a new state—a Quaker state, where he could govern in the way taught by Jesus Christ Himself. Penn found the King quite willing to further his plans, and a large tract of forest and prairie land in North America was granted to him. So fair did the land seem that he named it Sylvania, but the King, anxious to honour the name of the distinguished admiral, insisted on it being called Pennsylvania.

At once Penn set to work to found his holy kingdom; the watchwords of its government were to be Justice and Liberty. He had travelled throughout Europe, and had seen how kings and rulers used their power to get rich and more powerful, while the mass of the people were oppressed. Looking out on the world thus, reading his New Testament, and guided by the inner light of conscience, Penn felt called by God to show the nations the true and Christian way of government.

Carefully he framed laws that would ensure that the Spirit of Jesus Christ should have free and full course in the lives of all men, whose security and defence should be right-doing, and not weapons of war. Every man was to have freedom of conscience, and to be free from oppression and slavery. Sunday was to be observed as a sacred day. Above all, there was to be no militia or armed force, for either attack or defence.

Brothers—Red and White.

When Penn made known his rules for governing Pennsylvania he was laughed to scorn. Even the King was amused at his idea of trying to hold a colony in America without an army to defend it against the Indians. His plan to rule by the principles of the Sermon on the Mount was called foolish. People said he was mad, for it could not be done. As usual, however, Penn held on his way regardless of what men said, and busily prepared for his departure across the Atlantic, to set his new state going in person.

In October, 1682, a little barque named *The Welcome* reached the American coast, and Penn had his first glimpse of the New World from its deck. He landed at Newcastle, and was hailed with joy by the settlers. He chose a beautiful spot where two rivers met for his capital, finding his name for it in the New Testament— he called it Philadelphia, because the name meant brotherly love, and the Church there had been well spoken of by the angel in the Book of Revelation. The name was to be a lesson to its future inhabitants.

"Touching brotherly love, upon which I have come to these parts, and which I have shown to Dutch, Swedes, Indians and others alike," announced Penn, "I wish it may for ever characterise my new dominion."

Although granted this territory by the King of England, Penn bought the land from the Indians living on it. His next step was to arrange a treaty with them that would bind red man and white settler, without threats of force or display of weapons. He had conceived the bold plan of finding the security for his new settlers in a brotherly spirit between the races, instead of holding the red man in fear and subjection by a strong militia and a great show of warlike power. This was Penn's crowning folly in the eyes of the world.

Penn invited the sachems (the chief men of the Indian tribes) to meet him at Shackamaxon, which was their name for the spot he had renamed Philadelphia. Unarmed, and attended by a few other Quakers, Penn went out to meet them. His party was but a handful, and as far as the eye could reach the woods seemed alive with fierce-looking Indians in full war-paint, armed to the teeth with tomahawks, bows and arrows. In the centre of a forest glade stood a great elm tree, and under its spreading branches Penn waited for the Indian sachems to approach. In front of him were spread rolls of cloth and other gifts for the Indians. In his hand he held a roll of parchment, on which was written the treaty of purchase and friendship. As the Indians approached he put on his head a decorated headband. At this signal all the Indians threw down their weapons and seated themselves on the ground in a big half-circle. The chief then announced to Penn, through an interpreter, that the Indian nations were ready to hear him.

"The Great Spirit, Who knows the innermost thoughts of man, knows that I and my friends desire to live in peace and friendship with you, and to serve you to the utmost of our power," he said. "It is not our custom to use hostile weapons against our fellow-creatures, and for this reason we have come to you unarmed. Our object is not to do injury and thus provoke the Great Spirit, but to do good. We are now met on the broad pathway of good faith and good-will, so that no advantage is to be taken on either side, but all is to be openness, brotherhood, and love."

He then unrolled the parchment and explained the treaty clause by clause through an interpreter. As each clause was read the Indians made a great shout, which Penn took to be their way of saying Amen. Finally, turning to Penn and his party, the sachem described the future relations of the two parties in true Indian fashion :

" You are our brothers, and we will live like brothers with you. We will have a broad path for you and us to walk in. If an Englishman falls asleep in the path, the Indian shall pass him by, and say, ' He is our Englishman ; he is asleep, let him alone.' The path shall be plain ; there shall not be in it a stump to hurt the feet."

Without Militarism or Slavery.

William Penn made history that day. Not only was he a pioneer in taking no land from the Indians without paying for it, but the treaty of brotherhood was made without binding oath on either side. As a Quaker Penn refused at all times to swear on oath, deeming it unnecessary, since he always spoke the truth, and his word was his bond. As a matter of history, this treaty, unconfirmed by oath, was never broken. For more than seventy years no blood was shed between colonists and Indians in Pennsylvania ; not until the government had passed out of the hands of the Quakers was there war between Indian and Paleface, and even then it was not the Indians who first violated the treaty.

For some months after concluding his treaty with the Indians, Penn worked hard as governor of the state, helping his colonists to settle in, and arranging state affairs in such a way that it would be easy for his people to do right and hard for them to do evil.

Ten years later, Penn again sailed for the New World with his wife and children, probably expecting to end his days in the pioneer Christian state that he had founded there. As he set foot on Pennsylvanian soil he received a great welcome. The Governor was amazed and delighted with the great progress made by the settlers. Philadelphia, the capital, which he had planned out on his first visit, was now an attractive city with 700 houses and two Meeting Houses for worship. He at once travelled through the province, making speeches to his people, leading them in prayer, and putting right many things that had gone wrong during his absence in England. Wherever he went he was received with enthusiasm, but, unlike other colonial governors, he wore no grand uniform and had no military guard of honour.

One day a settler in the backwoods was surprised when a solitary stranger rode up to his door and begged shelter for the night. From his garb it was clear he was a Quaker, and the settler received the greatest surprise of his life when a chance remark of his guest led to the discovery that he was none other than the Governor himself. The settler's small boy was so full of curiosity and amazement that after the Governor had retired for the night the boy crept up the stairs and peeped through the keyhole of the great man's bedroom. His unpardonable curiosity was turned to awe as he saw the Governor on his knees in earnest prayer by the bedside, and could hear him thanking God for His goodness, and praying for peace and blessing on all in the house.

Sometimes the Governor turned preacher, and rode through Pennsylvania as an ordinary minister of the Gospel. He also practised the teaching of Jesus Christ by many simple acts of friendliness.

One day he was riding to a small settlement to join the people in their worship, and chanced to overtake a little girl on the road. She was obviously very poor and wore neither shoes nor stockings. Reining in his horse he greeted her in friendly fashion.

" Whither art thou going, little maid ? "

" To meeting," replied the girl shyly, not knowing who the stranger was. At once he stopped his horse and helped her to climb up behind him, to give her a lift on the journey. That morning the citizens were amazed to see the Governor ride into their midst with a poor child riding behind him, her bare legs dangling over the horse's flanks.

For two years Penn stayed in Pennsylvania, working very hard to make his people happy and prosperous. In particular he sought to abolish slavery from the colony. " The buying, selling and holding men in slavery is inconsistent with the tenets of the Christian religion," he declared. Under his leadership the Quakers not only began to treat their slaves better than others, but admitted them into their worship as brothers.

Frequently he travelled far to the camping grounds of the Indians, to make treaties of friendship with new tribes. Some of these tribes, as they wandered from province to province, had met other governors and white men, who had proved anything but their friends. Imagine their surprise when the Governor of Pennsylvania came into their camp unarmed, wanting to make a covenant of brotherhood with them. Sitting on the ground amongst them during their feasts, sharing their venison, and eating their hot-cakes of wheat and beans, no wonder that they were ready to trust this Governor. On one occasion forty chiefs met him to make a treaty of brotherhood, and agreed " by their hands and seals to be as one head and one heart, and to live in true friendship and amity as one people."

Although the Christian state founded by Penn, and known as his " holy experiment," eventually passed into the hands of the British Government, and sank to the level of an ordinary state, his work was not in vain. His plan of ruling by justice and love can never be improved upon, and to-day people are seeing more and more that right is better than might, that love is stronger than hate, and that to preserve peace may demand far more courage than going to war.

NOTES ON THE YARN.

Aim.

To show how William Penn, through prayer and obedience to the inner light of conscience, became the champion of religious liberty and as a Christian Governor founded a model state.

Biographical.

The life story of few men would better illustrate the power of prayer in practical affairs than the career of William Penn. His daily habit of communing with God in prayer led him to deep spiritual experiences. More important still for the world, his prayer-life led him to great spiritual discoveries of the will of God for man. It was through prayer that he became the pioneer in a new attitude towards native races. With a boldness born of religious knowledge, he dared to trust the Red Indians, even to the point of going unarmed into their country, and contrary to general expectation these spiritual methods worked. To the Indians, Penn appeared as a new sort of white man, whose benign countenance and gentle manner won their confidence, even while his iron will and stern sense of duty commanded their respect. The secret of Penn's personality, which counted so much on these occasions, was his habit of " practising the presence of God," ever seeking to walk by the inner light, through prayer.

William Penn was born in London on 14th October, 1644. His father, Admiral William Penn, has been called " one of the suppressed characters in English history," for, like Admiral Blake, to whom he alone stood second, the story of his work has never been told. Inheriting his father's courage and strong will, young Penn's religious character developed early. At eleven he had a strange religious experience that constituted a clear call to the religious life. He soon discovered that he had a strong spiritual affinity to George Fox and his followers. The Society of Friends, called Quakers, were at this time coming into prominence, and Penn believed that it was by Divine plan that he was brought again and again into contact with this despised and persecuted sect. His religious experience made him a successful minister and champion of the Friends, and he became a sturdy defender for the rights of free speech and religious liberty ; in managing his father's estates he proved himself a successful man of affairs ; as the son of the King's friend he became the Court favourite of an unpopular monarch, who was a Papist. After-events proved that he was very unwise in attaching himself so prominently to James II., but viewing his life as a whole, we cannot escape the conclusion that, despite his critics, he remained a man of untarnished honour. As the proprietor and Governor of Pennsylvania, he proved a pioneer Christian administrator, drawing up a constitution that no statesman of his day could match. Penn's state was based on Christian principles, and his success proves for all time that the Sermon on the Mount is practical. To the utmost of his powers he stopped the exploitation of both Red Indians and Negroes, and his treaty with the Indians proved for seventy years that peace and brotherhood is a surer defence than sword or gunpowder. His later years were clouded by adversity, and after his final return to England in 1701 his deputy in Pennsylvania practically ruined him by his villainy. Penn refused to pay false claims brought against him, and was thrown into the Fleet Prison in 1708, where his sufferings so undermined his constitution that memory and understanding failed him, and he died on July 30th, 1718.

Questions.

Why did Penn act in defiance of his father's wishes ?
What made him a " Nonconformist " ?
Why did he found a colony in America ?
How was it different from other states and colonies ?
How did Penn prove a pioneer of the League of Nations ?
How would his method abolish war and misery ?
Where did he get his inspiration and ideals for his " Holy Experiment " ?

VIII

WILLIAM TYNDALE

Dates : B., about 1484 *: D.,* 1536.

"THE BIBLE IN OUR MOTHER-TONGUE"

On top of the Cotswold Hills a boy lay watching the
long view westwards. In the distance were the blue
hills of Wales, but the centre of attraction was the silvery
waters of the Severn, threading its way to the narrow
seas. Probably the boy did not know that a hundred
years earlier those silvery waters had borne to the ocean
the ashes of John Wycliffe.

The boy was William Tyndale, whose name was to
become linked for ever with that of John Wycliffe in
the story of the English Bible. When the day came
for him to go to Oxford, he came under the spell of John
Colet, afterwards the famous Dean of St. Paul's. As
Colet lectured on the Bible and opened up the meaning
of the Scriptures to his students, young Tyndale was
drawn more and more to the study of the sacred page.

Before long he moved on to the sister university at
Cambridge. The magnet that drew him thither was the
famous Erasmus, greatest of the English schoolmen,
at that very time hard at work translating the New
Testament into modern Greek. Tyndale's interest in
the Bible developed greatly under the influence of
Erasmus, and it may be that he heard the great scholar
express that wish of his that has become famous :

" I wish that even the weakest woman might read the Gospels and the Epistles of St. Paul. . . . I long for the day when the husbandman shall sing portions of them to himself as he follows the plough, when the weaver shall hum them to the time of his shuttle, when the traveller shall wile away with their stories the weariness of his journey."

That noble wish must have been echoed in Tyndale's heart, for he came to realise that the only remedy for the ignorance and evil lives of the people of his day was to give them the New Testament in their own language. So we find him turning Erasmus's fine new Greek version into an English New Testament. This work was begun at Little Sodbury, on the Cotswolds, not far from his birthplace, where he was serving as chaplain to the lord of the manor. Nor for long was he allowed to work in peace. Bishops and priests soon discovered that this chaplain was a " heretic," not only holding " wicked " opinions in favour of giving the Bible to the people, but engaged on the " evil " work of translating it into common speech !

One day there was an exciting scene in a public debate about the study of the Bible between a priest and Tyndale.

" We had better be without God's laws than the Pope's," declared the priest piously.

Up jumped Tyndale, stirred to indignant wrath at such blasphemy.

" I defy the Pope and all his laws," he declared, " and if God spares me, I will one day make the boy that drives the plough in England to know more of Scripture than the Pope does."

Such a magnificent vow would have cost Tyndale his life had he remained at Little Sodbury, so he fled to London, believing that Bishop Tonstall was a man of light and leading, and would give him shelter and protection for his work. Alas for his hopes ! The

Bishop received him coolly and would give him no help. Undaunted, he turned to the pulpit and began to read his English version to the people in one of the London churches. Among his congregation was a wealthy London merchant, Humphrey Monmouth, who gladly gave Tyndale a home and all the help he needed to continue his work.

Forced into Exile.

For twelve months he worked quietly at his task ; then he took warning from events that were going on around him and prepared to flee once more. He knew that if his precious sheets of the English New Testament could be secured by the servants of the Pope, they would be instantly destroyed, and his life would be forfeit. Of personal danger he cared nothing, but he was determined to save his precious manuscripts, so he chose to become an exile.

" I perceived that not only in my Lord of London's palace, but in all England, there was no room for attempting a translation of the Scriptures," he wrote sadly.

So it came about that in May, 1524, Tyndale secretly boarded a vessel bound for Hamburg, and a few hours later saw the shores of his native land dropping quickly out of sight behind him. Then began years of suffering, labour, and peril. In poverty, in exile from his native land, in bitter absence from his friends, in hunger and thirst, in cold, in constant danger from the spies of the Pope, who were everywhere, he plodded on, making his home finally in Antwerp, where several wealthy English merchants lived who were favourable to his plans.

Day after day, and far into each night, he worked feverishly on, while the pile of closely-written sheets of his English New Testament grew higher and higher. Always he was in deadly fear, not for his life, but lest his precious sheets should be seized by the enemy. Within twelve months, such was his energy, his work was finished. Then arose a new difficulty and a far greater peril. More fortunate than Wycliffe, the invention of printing made him independent of copyists. Once he could get his English New Testament printed, thousands of copies could be sent into England. But where could he find a printer bold enough to risk such dangerous work ? And how could the printing be kept so secret that the work could be finished without the spies of the Pope knowing anything about it ? In only a few cities as yet was the art of printing established. By careful inquiry he discovered a printer at Cologne who might undertake the hazards of the task. Packing up his precious documents he secretly journeyed thither.

The English Testament Printed !

A few evenings later, in the gloom of twilight, the Cologne printer was surprised by the call of a mysterious visitor enshrouded in a long black cloak, his features half-hidden by a large hat drawn well down on his face. Glancing round furtively to make sure they were alone, the visitor produced a large bundle and boldly asked the printer's aid in this hazardous enterprise of printing the first English New Testament. To Tyndale's great joy the task was accepted, and next day, after pledging his compositor to secrecy, the printer began his work. Behind locked doors and away from prying eyes Tyndale's manuscript was set up in type. In the dead of night the mysterious visitor came regularly to read the proof sheets and superintend the printing work.

For a time all went well. Then the pride of the compositor got the better of his prudence.

" Things are going on in my master's printing shop that will soon make the people of England rub their eyes in astonishment!'' boasted the man to his friends in an inn.

A spying priest, John Cochlaus, overheard the boast and in friendly fashion plied the man with wine that loosened his tongue, and Tyndale's secret was discovered. In the providence of God an inkling of what had happened reached the ears of Tyndale in his lodgings. Half-distracted and thoroughly alarmed, he rushed to the printer's house, seized his manuscript and as many of the printed sheets as he could carry, and fled from the town.

Guided by the hand of God, as he afterwards declared, Tyndale went straight to Worms, where Martin Luther had already found shelter. Here he found a printer ready to help him, and within a short time he had the intense joy of taking into his hands the first completed copy of the English Testament. Then began the difficult and dangerous task of smuggling copies of the forbidden book into England. Here he had the help of the English merchants at Antwerp, with the result that before long hundreds of copies of the English Testament were carried secretly into England, concealed in bales of merchandise. So eager were the English people for the Gospel that copies could not be printed fast enough for them. In a short time it is reckoned that 6,000 copies were printed and smuggled into England.

The English bishops and priests at once took alarm. A hundred years earlier it had been easy to trace out and destroy copies of Wycliffe's Bible that had been laboriously written by hand. But to stamp out a book that was being brought into the country by the hundred was no easy matter, the more so because the printing press at Worms was producing more copies every day. Vigorous measures were at once taken to cope with what was regarded as a terrible evil. Every port was carefully watched by the officers of the bishops ; the circulation and reading of the Testaments was prohibited, and all copies seized were publicly burned with solemn ceremony as " a burnt offering most pleasing to Almighty God."

The news that his precious Testaments were being destroyed in large numbers failed to discourage Tyndale. Rather was it a challenge to produce more and better versions ! While the printing press was kept busy, Tyndale worked on trying to improve the translation.

" In burning the book," he said, " they did none other thing than I looked for ; no more shall they do if they burn me also, if it be God's will that it should be so."

So in spite of Pope and priests the supply of Testaments never failed, and Tyndale and his friends were ever at pains to discover fresh ways of smuggling them past the spies that watched at every English port. In cases, in barrels, hidden in bales of cloth and in sacks of flour, the books went into England, and although many were discovered and burned triumphantly, many more escaped detection and were scattered far and wide throughout the land.

Burning the Bible

One of the chief factors that controlled the output of Tyndale's printing press was money, for in those early days of printing it was an expensive process. One day financial help came from an unexpected source. A London merchant, newly arrived from the homeland, greeted the translator with the welcome news :

" Master Tyndale, I have found you a good purchaser for your books."

" Who is he ? " asked Tyndale eagerly.

" My lord the Bishop of London ! " was the triumphant reply.

" But if the Bishop wants the books," said the puzzled Tyndale, " it must be only to burn them."

" Well, what of that ? " said the merchant, "the

bishop will burn them anyhow, and it is best that you should have the money for printing others instead."

With great glee the merchant told Tyndale how Bishop Tonstall had come to him one day with a brilliant idea for stopping the smuggling of Bibles into England. Not knowing that this merchant was a friend of Tyndale's, the Bishop arranged for the purchase of all the copies obtainable at Antwerp, saying :

"Do your diligence and get them for me, and I will gladly give you whatever they may cost. For the books are naughty, and I intend surely to destroy them all, and to burn them at Paul's Cross."

Thus it came about that numbers of copies of the English Bible fell into the hands of the Bishop, who was delighted with the success of his scheme. Little did he know that the money he freely spent in this way was being used by Tyndale to set up new type. The translator had been hard at work improving his New Testament, but up till that time had been unable to print this better edition for want of money. So the Bishop's scheme for buying all the Bibles before they could reach England had the effect of putting a new and better edition in great numbers on the market—thus helping the work of Tyndale immensely.

As a result of the Bishop's activity there were regular Bible burnings outside St. Paul's Cathedral, and these caused such a stir among the citizens of London that more people than ever wanted to buy the book and read it for themselves. The Bible burnings thus became the best form of advertisement for Tyndale's work.

Not long afterwards a heretic was on his trial before Sir Thomas More. The man was accused of helping the work of Tyndale by passing on copies of the banned book. Anxious to discover how so much expensive printing could be done, Sir Thomas made a bargain with the heretic, promising to show him favour if he would confess who it was that was helping Tyndale by providing the money for his work.

" My lord," said the man readily, " I will tell thee truly—it is the Bishop of London who hath helped us ! "

When Bishop Tonstall, Sir Thomas More, and others realised that they could not destroy Tyndale's work by buying or burning his New Testaments, they tried a new plan. Preaching at Paul's Cross to a great congregation, Tonstall declared that not only was Tyndale's Testament a naughty book, but that it was full of errors. After denouncing and ridiculing it, he held a copy on high for all to see, and then flung it into a fire that was burning near.

Sir Thomas More also took a hand in decrying Tyndale's translation.

" To study to find errors in Tyndale's book were like studying to find water in the sea," he said. " The book is too bad even to be mended ; for it is easier to make web of new cloth than it is to sew up every hole in a net."

These attacks drew a prompt reply from Tyndale, who proved that the errors could be narrowed down to about half-a-dozen mistranslated words.

Betrayed and Martyred.

In poverty, exile, and the bitter absence of his friends, Tyndale worked on through the years to complete his revised New Testament, and also to give to his people the Old Testament. He made his home in Antwerp, a free city, where he was perfectly safe from his enemies. Not content with this work, he wrote tracts and books to expose the errors of the Pope and his priests, and to urge the people to take the Bible for their guide in life. He kept two days a week free for his " pastime," as he called it, of visiting poor English exiles who had taken refuge in Antwerp from persecution at home. Every Monday and Saturday found him searching the streets and poorer parts of the city, seeking all who were in need of help.

Although Sir Thomas More was not above calling him a beast, his enemies could prove nothing against his character, and his life at Antwerp showed that he shared Wycliffe's view that " he hath need to live a clean life and a devout who undertook to translate the Bible."

To get him into their power they tried to persuade him to return to England, and made many promises of safety, but he was too cautious to be taken in. Their next move was to send a treacherous priest, Henry Phillips, to betray him into their hands. Phillips went about his work all too well, and Tyndale's generosity and kindness of heart proved to be his undoing. Pretending to be in need, Phillips induced Tyndale, whose generous nature refused to listen to his landlord's suspicions, to lend him money. On a pretended errand of mercy he was lured far from his house, then treacherously seized by Phillips' confederates, hurried out of the safety of Antwerp, and thrown into the dungeons of the Castle of Vilvorde. Here he was within the domain of the Pope, and could expect no mercy. As the year advanced the poor prisoner, in his misery and rags, sent a begging letter to the Governor :

" Be kind enough to send me from my goods which are in your possession a warmer cap ; a warmer coat also, for that which I have is very thin ; also a piece of cloth to patch my leggings. My shirts, too, are worn out."

He asked also for his books, so that he might continue his work, but it was not to be. Early in October he was taken outside his prison, chained to the stake, strangled and burnt, his last words being a fervent prayer : " Lord, open the King of England's eyes."

Priests, bishops, and Pope rejoiced when they learned that at last Tyndale was out of their way. But their triumph was short-lived ! Within three years of his

death and by order of the King, the English Bible—
completed by Tyndale before his death—was being placed
in every parish church in England. The battle for an
open Bible was won.

NOTES ON THE YARN

Aim.

To show how Tyndale devoted his life to giving us the first printed
English Bible.

Biographical.

The greatest monument to the character and achievement of William
Tyndale is our English Bible. In spite of all the advantages of modern
scholarship and culture, Tyndale's work was so well and truly done that
many chapters, particularly of the New Testament, differ only in the
turn of a phrase from the revised version of 1885. The historian, Froude,
suggests that he laid the foundation on which all subsequent revisions
have been built, and says : " The peculiar genius which breathes through
it, the mingled tenderness and majesty, the Saxon simplicity, the preter-
natural grandeur unequalled and unapproached in the attempted improve-
ments of modern scholars—all are here, and bear the impress of the mind
of one man—William Tyndale." The secret of this was not only his skill
in languages and his great capacity for hard work, but in the fact that he
lived in the spirit of the Divine Word. Seeking to make the Book an
inspiration and a guide to others, he tried to live up to its high standard.
" My conscience beareth me record." he wrote in the preface of his 1526
New Testament, " that of a pure intent, singly and faithfully I have
interpreted it, as far as God gave me the gift of knowledge and understanding." Little wonder, then, that Jowett, Master of Balliol, could
say of a work that sprang from his, " In a certain sense the Authorised
Version was more inspired than the original."

William Tyndale was born about 1484, probably at Melksham Court,
Stinchcombe, Glos., and studied at Magdalen Hall, Oxford, graduating
B.A. there in 1512. Here he probably came under the influence of John
Colet, but later was attracted to Cambridge by the fame of Erasmus.
In 1521 he became chaplain and tutor to Sir John Walsh, of Little
Sodbury, Glos., but his sympathies with the new learning made his removal
to London a wise precaution. After two years work on his English New
Testament under the patronage of Humphrey Monmouth, he fled to
Hamburg in 1524, then probably went to Wittenburg to confer with
Martin Luther. In 1525, at Cologne, with the help of a Franciscan friar
named William Roye, he began with Quentel the printing of his English
New Testament, with a first impression of three thousand copies quarto.
No sooner had Matthew and Mark been printed than discovery by a papal
spy, John Cochlaeus, forced him to flee to Worms. Here Peter Schoeffer
started printing a new impression in small octavo, without prefaces or
marginal notes. When this was done Quentel's quarto Bible was completed, with introduction and marginal references. In his translation

Tyndale owed much to Luther and to Erasmus's Greek Testament. By 1530 six editions, numbering about 15,000 copies, had been printed and surreptitiously distributed—yet so fierce and systematic was the persecution of the book that no single complete copy exists, the nearest being a copy of the first octavo (with only the title page missing), preserved in the Baptist College at Bristol. Later Tyndale published his version of the Pentateuch, the Book of Jonah, and large portions from the Old Testament and the Apocrypha. He also revised his New Testament several times. He found sanctuary for this work in Antwerp, where neither Henry the Eighth nor the Pope could harm him. He was betrayed by Henry Phillips on 24th May, 1535, with the help of some of the bishops. For sixteen months he lay in the castle of Vilvorde, and apparently Thomas Cromwell tried to save him. Before his martyrdom he had completed the Old Testament to the end of Chronicles. After a protracted trial he was condemned for heresy, and strangled and burnt on Friday, October 6th, 1536.

Possibly Tyndale's last days were gladdened by the knowledge that Miles Coverdale, who had helped him in Hamburg in 1529, had printed the first complete English Bible; and that King Henry VIII. had severed all connection with the Pope of Rome. In 1537 appeared the first Bible actually printed in England, known as " Matthew's Bible," edited by John Rogers, another friend and helper of Tyndale, and containing all Tyndale's work combined with that of Coverdale. In 1539 the " great Bible " was printed under Coverdale's superintendence, and ordered to be set up in parish churches throughout the land. Thus, 111 years after the ashes of Wycliffe had been borne into the Severn, and three years after Tyndale had won the crown of martyrdom, the supremacy of the Bible was acknowledged in all England.

Questions.

Why did Tyndale begin to translate the New Testament ?
What made him leave England ?
Why did he suffer hardship and face danger in order to get his New Testament completed and printed ?
What do we owe to him to-day ?
What is the place the Bible should occupy in our lives ?

Made and Printed in Great Britain by
Cox & Wyman, Ltd., London, Fakenham and Reading